The New Americans
Recent Immigration and American Society

Edited by
Steven J. Gold and Rubén G. Rumbaut

A Series from LFB Scholarly

Immigrant Children Negotiate School
The Border in Our Hearts

Donna Vukelich-Selva

LFB Scholarly Publishing LLC
El Paso 2014

Copyright © 2014 by LFB Scholarly Publishing LLC

Library of Congress Cataloging-in-Publication Data

Vukelich-Selva, Donna, 1958-
  Immigrant children negotiate school : the border in our hearts / Donna Vukelich-Selva.
     pages cm. -- (The New Americans: Recent Immigration and American Society)
  Includes bibliographical references and index.
  ISBN 978-1-59332-700-2 (hardcover : alk. paper)
  1. Latin Americans--Education--United States. 2. Latin American students--United States--Social conditions. 3. Immigrant children--Education--United States. 4. Immigrant children--United States--Social conditions. I. Title.
  LC2670.V85 2014
  371.829'68073--dc23

                                     2013051155

ISBN 978-1-59332-700-2

Printed on acid-free 250-year-life paper.

Manufactured in the United States of America.

In memory of my father, George Andrew Vukelich, 1927-1995, who went to elementary school without speaking a word of English and later become a formidable force of nature with a pen. And in honor of my mother, Helen Gutensohn Vukelich, who has always managed to be on the right side of things.

All honor, always, to the amazing students of Room 134.

Table of Contents

Preface

This book offers a snapshot of the Latino students in one classroom at what I will call Prairie Heights, a high school in the upper Midwest. While Latino students are an ever-more important population in schools across the nation's heartland, we rarely hear their voices. This is not a scientific study, but rather a series of stories, each important in itself and each critical for educators and others who are committed to their Latino students and who embrace the multilingual, multicultural communities that make schools today truly vibrant and exciting places. I have tried to honor their voices and place their stories in the larger historical and contemporary context of immigrant students and education, as I worked to understand the crucial ways that race, culture and legal status impact student identity and success.

With much gratitude to the ongoing inspiration provided by so many scholars whose work has influenced me and provided both context and foundation. Michael Apple, Gloria Ladson-Billings and Ben Marquez were all influential in shaping the way I understand education and immigration, and I am grateful for their teaching excellence as well. I have learned much from other scholars, including Angela Valenzuela, Pedro Noguera, Jeff Duncan-Andrade, Bekisiswe Ndimande, Maria Elena Ramirez, Adrienne Dixson and Guadalupe Valdes, and thank them for continuing to offer insight and hope.

With much respect to those who continue to fight for just and vibrant public schools for *all* students in Wisconsin, including Alfonso Zepeda-Capistrán, TJ Mertz, Bob Peterson, Rebecca Kemble, Bert Zipperer, Veronica Castillo, and Elizabeth Miller.

My eternal appreciation to treasured colleagues and friends, with thanks for their perspectives and wisdom: Susan Pastor, Patricia Castañeda-Tucker, Jennifer Hull, Karyn Rotker, Denise Hanson, Jed

Hopkins, Tony Garcia, Dana Hagerman, Rebecca Zambrano, Sheila Hopkins and John Kibler.

Love and gratitude to Claudio, and special thanks to my two sons, Jorge Fernando and Joaquín Andrés—just by being, they have taught me more than I would have imagined possible.

All errors, of course, are mine (and perhaps, like some handcrafted items, the flaws within signify authenticity).

Introduction

School and the Borderlands

The long, unforgiving border separating Mexico and the US is both materially and symbolically potent, and the increasing fluidity of that border is changing much of what continues to be referred to as "America".[1] As the United States and its schools adjust to the 21st century, a demographic shift of far-reaching proportions continues to change school districts throughout the country. In recent years, the border's reach has extended far beyond its traditional boundaries, demanding that all those affected by this ongoing change, including those of us who are educators, redraw our sense of this country's boundaries and how they affect our students.

When I returned to the US after 15 years in Central America, where I taught for many years, I hoped to examine the ways in which the massive implementation of neoliberal policies was transforming education in that region already devastated by years of war. Yet it soon became clear to me that even in the upper Midwest, this global south has a palpable presence, one that is having a profound impact on education, as it transforms entire communities and the public schools in particular. Many public schools, like those in the Lakeview district where I carried out my research, have faced deepening budget cuts, increasing numbers of students with special needs and, perhaps most significantly, a demographic sea change as scores of Latino[2] immigrant

---

[1] I do not generally use the terms "America" or "American", as all the students I worked with during my research can rightfully call themselves "Americans", and come from one part of the Americas. Thus, I have chosen to use either the United States or the US.

[2] I use "Latino" to be inclusive of all, and not specific to one gender.

children alter the historically homogenous make-up of many schools. This transition has been the subject of massive commentary and controversy in the media and, to a certain degree, in academic discourse as well. The students I taught in Central America and their peers from Mexico and South America, are now found in almost every school throughout the upper Midwest. While in some ways they are quite similar to earlier immigrants and even to those immigrants from other parts of the world[3] who share their classrooms, hallways, and often their neighborhoods, there are also key distinctions. The students I encountered in the Midwest, although at an enormous physical distance from the border, have not left that border behind them. In many ways, they *are* the border. That border informs their lives and is absolutely crucial to the ways in which they construct their academic identities. It is also a real, living entity in their lives and frames those lives in a very different way than those of earlier immigrant students in the upper Midwest where my study takes place.

Most of the more than 12 million immigrants who entered the United States in the 60-some years that Ellis Island served as the key immigrant port of entry did not have the economic wherewithal to even think about going back to the 'old country,' nor, of course, did they have access to the kind of technology that facilitates ongoing communication. My grandmother, who arrived at Ellis Island in the early 1920s, had a small wooden box in which she kept a pile of photographs and letters written in Romanian and Serbo-Croatian from her family and my grandfather's, heartfelt attempts to keep contact with the family they knew they would never see again. She and many others like here were desperate to become 'American'[4] at almost any cost, and they embraced the possibility of making it in this new country with a particular energy and singlemindedness. For many Eastern and Southern Europeans who faced much racism as they arrived in the US, becoming "American" often meant becoming "white" and a key

---

[3] Students at Prairie Heights, the high school where I carried out my research, come from over 50 countries, and reflect in many ways the shifting patterns of human movement around the globe.

[4] Unfortunately, this often meant that the children born to these immigrants lost their native language, and sometimes other cultural markers as well.

element of assimilation was clearly choosing racial allegiances (a "choice" that was dependent on where you came from and what you looked like), as well as buying uncritically into the mythology of US opportunity and largess. These immigrants also dutifully sent their children off to the public schools, a central element of the push by the US government to ensure a measure of shared experience and knowledge among its new citizens.

The many Mexican immigrants who came to the US in the 20th century were faced with a school system that was often brutal in its attempt to 'Americanize' their children. (San Miguel, 1987; Sánchez, 1993) A wave of political organizing and resistance responded to these attempts, and we are clearly in the midst of another such wave today. The Mexican immigrants in the upper Midwest and, indeed, throughout the country, are generally quite clear about their desire to maintain a cultural identity even as they seek to embrace and understand their new culture.[5] Though that has been feasible, to a degree, in areas with large Latino populations, it was often quite difficult in smaller communities throughout the US.

My research considers several intertwined threads of a story currently unfolding in a number of small communities across the nation. In the late 1990s and early part of this century, with the Mexican economy facing severe strain and the so-called drug war taking an increasing toll, more and more Mexicans headed North to find work. Historically, of course, this flow of immigrants is nothing new. What marks a relatively new phase is that now many of the immigrants end up not only in the regions geographically bordering Mexico, but also all over the country, including small towns and cities throughout the upper Midwest. Mexican immigrants have always been essential to the US economy, and immigration has been ongoing for more than a century, oftentimes at the behest of US companies who went deep into Mexico to recruit cheap labor. Immigrants were particularly affected by changes, whether ripples or major convulsions, in the US economy and have historically been used, or more precisely exploited, when they were needed, with both companies and the

---

[5]In fact, in many ways, this new wave of immigration has created a culture of its own – mixing language and other cultural markers to reflect the fluidity of the situation that is their reality.

government turning a blind eye to immigration regulations. The harsh flip side is that immigrants have also been under near constant attack, and the 20th century saw waves of massive deportations (Balderrama and Rodriguez, 2006), with no due process, as well as outbreaks of violence and harassment, whenever the US economy was in trouble and easy and accessible scapegoats were needed. Since the events of 9/11, immigrants have come under even more scrutiny, and the ongoing recession has only compounded the difficulties immigrants face. During Barack Obama's first term, a record 1.5 million people were deported and deportations and detentions continue to be high into his second term.

The 1980s saw an unprecedented upswing in immigration from Central America, due to US policy aimed at destabilizing the Sandinista government in Nicaragua and shoring up the military dictatorships in El Salvador and Guatemala. The massive devaluation of the *peso* in Mexico in the early 1980s also caused a spike in Mexican immigration, but it was the passage of the North American Free Trade Act (NAFTA, enacted in 1994) and the subsequent devastating impact on the Mexican economy that brought a new surge in immigration to the US. Many of those immigrants ended up in towns and across the upper Midwest, where in many cases they were a new and unknown population. As those communities change, of course, so do their schools. Not surprisingly, perhaps, that change is not always welcomed, and rarely understood.

The new 'wave' of immigration is also markedly different in that today's immigrants are able to do something that is historically somewhat unusual – keep up close ties with their homes. While it would be absurd to claim that today's immigrants have it easy, it is important to recognize that there is a certain amount of agency in the very fact of mobility, particularly given the explosion of technology that makes it possible for a young Mexican immigrant in a small town to talk to his or her cousins, using social media. At the same time, today's immigrants from Mexico and Central America are quite vulnerable and subject to both a legal and political backlash against their presence here. Even as both major political parties in the US point to the Latino vote as decisive in the 2012 presidential elections, there is not much agreement, let alone consensus, about what the next political steps should be.

In one example of immigrant experiences in the Lakeview school district, Hmong families (the second largest group of immigrants in the district) have done much to maintain their language and cultural traditions, often in the fact of much ignorance and sometimes opposition from the schools. An important distinction is that they do not have the possibility of ever going back "home"; the children who are school age today either grew up in the US or refugee camps, and although they often grow up with the strong pull of culture and tradition, on some level it is quite out of reach for them.[6] Not insignificantly, it has also given them legal documents, an issue whose enormity becomes clear as one hears story after story from students who fear that legal status is forever out of reach.

I began my research out of a concern to understand what leads to the poor achievement rates of Latino students in the Lakeview school district.[7] When I returned to the US, I became involved in some community initiatives promoting Latino student success and was dismayed by the bleak statistics I encountered. About 37% of all Latino students in the Lakeview school district today do not graduate, and some of the district's standard measuring sticks are not consistently administered to second-language students, making a clear picture of achievement difficult to bring into focus. The graduation rates give only a partial sense of where students are, as many of the Latino students at Prairie Heights are far less prepared for post-secondary studies than their White counterparts. About 75% of the school's White students take the ACT, with an average composite score of 27.5.

---

[6] Many of the students I worked with spoke frequently about going back to Mexico as one option after high school. Several had visited Mexico, though this is not possible for most as they do not have legal documentation to be in the US and so cannot take the risk of leaving and then being unable to return.

[7] When I began my research, nearly half of all Latino students did not graduate. Latino student performance on the state standardized tests shows 41% at a "minimal" level, while 31% posted scores that were "basic", 22% scored as "proficient" and only 5% were "advanced". Over 80% of White students at Prairie Heights scored at the advanced level, while only 3% were "minimal".

Just over 40% of Latino students at Prairie Heights take the ACT, and their average composite score is 22.

Because I believe so strongly in the power and authenticity of narrative, my research attempts to *contar las historias de los sin voz*, that is, to recount the stories of the voiceless – the immigrant students of room 134. In honoring these stories, I stand firmly in the tradition of the *testimonio*[8] of Latin America. This, of course, is also a fundamental underpinning of Critical Race Theory, which offers the very useful concept of counter-storytelling. This study focuses on some of the students at Prairie Heights, one of the high schools where the young people of these immigrant families end up. While I will look specifically at the stories of Latino youth as students, my telling of their stories inevitably calls on their particular strands of a larger immigrant narrative. I examine the ways in which Latino students experience school, and identify those factors that are central to ensuring that students are able to be successful as students, as well as indicating some factors that thwart, or block, their success. I ask the following questions: How do issues of cultural, racial and linguistic identity play out in the daily school lives of the Latino students at Prairie Heights? What causes students to identify with the school and want to be part of it, as compared with those whose identity is tied up in *not* doing well in school? How do the existing power dynamics in the school specifically affect these students?

This study considers the ways in which students begin to understand themselves as students, not removed or distanced from the border, but firmly located in the context of that border as a very clearly drawn boundary along which they are forced to walk. From my vantage point as a researcher, I was able to see the many resources that these students could potentially contribute to the broader community, thus offering some insight into the shifting face of public education, and the challenges that lie ahead. The stories that I heard in room 134 are shaped to a certain degree by the fact that the students telling them find themselves in a small university town in the Upper Midwest where

---

[8]*Testimonio* comes out of the Latin and Central American context and actively encourages a narrative of witness, recognizing as valid and worthy of study the lived experiences of those not usually considered as protagonists of history.

they, while increasingly visible, are largely unseen. At the end of a large march for immigrant rights in the spring of the second year I was at Prairie Heights, several White bystanders were openly wondering, "Where did all these Latinos *come* from?" Ironically, that sentiment was echoed by some of the students, as voiced by Domingo[9], whom I had seen at the march, but was not close enough to actually speak with. "Miss," he said the next day, prefacing his conversation with the typical salutation used by most of the students, whether or not they were speaking in Spanish or English. "Miss, I didn't know *we* were so many".

THE COMMUNITY

The students in room 134 at Prairie Heights High School attend school in a small city, and understanding that community's sense of itself is absolutely necessary to recognizing what has happened to its students. Lakeview is a small city in the upper Midwest. The largest employers in the area are a large public university, several small colleges and the state government. Historically, the city has been fairly racially homogeneous, and even today the city is about 80% white. A contentious urban renewal program in the 1960s razed the city's most racially mixed neighborhood (a mix of Italian, African American and Jewish residents, much remembered with both nostalgia for the days gone by and anger at what happened to the community), which was the only place that non-Whites in Lakeview could easily find a place to live. The one remaining traditional African American neighborhood is fairly poor. Rapid growth on the city's outskirts, along with major influxes of Hmong refugees[10], began to change the city's school population in the early 1980s. Those changes came on the heels of a federally-mandated school desegregation order which transformed a number of Lakeview's neighborhood schools through a busing program that continues today.

---

[9]None of the names I use to refer to students are their real names.

[10]The Hmong people fought on the side of the United States during the Vietnam War and many were killed or ended up in refugee camps in Thailand after the war ended in 1975. Thousands of Hmong were allowed to enter the US as refugees and beginning in the 1980s, many came to the upper Midwest.

In the last 15-20 years, many Mexican and Central American workers have come to the city, seeking better economic and educational opportunities than those they left in their countries. Immigrant Latino families makes up an increasingly important sector to the area's workforce, oftentimes in virtually invisible jobs, barely making ends meet. While the city is 80% White, not quite half of the Lakeview district's students are White. Some of that difference may be explained by different birth rates across racial groups, but there has clearly been an observable amount of "white flight"—in this case, many families have stayed in the city itself, but have pulled their children from the public schools. Since the early 1980s, several private schools have been founded, including a few evangelical Christian schools, and a few of the longstanding Catholic schools have built substantial new additions as they scramble to meet the increasing demand.

The Lakeview school district is proud of its schools and, in fact, many families would second that assessment. The community's longstanding, if somewhat exaggerated, reputation as an open-minded, progressive community is a source of particular pride to the school district and is explicitly referred to in materials published by the district. Yet, the picture is often more complicated. The increasing numbers of Latinos have caused some conflict in the community. In the late 1990s, several city parks cracked down on small groups of Latino adult males (not teenagers) who gathered in the parks to socialize. Letters to a local newspaper noted that while these men came under surveillance by the police, the Saturday tailgaters for collegiate sporting events, including many in those same parks, did not; in fact, they were portrayed in the local media as fun-loving sports fans. This kind of racial profiling caused much concern and the Lakeview police department has responded by working to hire more Latino and Spanish-speaking officers and increasing its outreach to the Latino community. When young Latino men were arrested for fighting or possible gang activity, a storm of angry comments on local media sites inevitably followed, quickly degenerating into immigrant bashing, with many racial slurs. One Central American immigrant professional noted a sign on a local, public golf course that had been altered to read "no dogs or Mexicans allowed." He snapped a photo to show to disbelieving White colleagues who were simply unable to fathom that this sort of thing could happen in their town.

Thus we see that the new immigrant communities in Lakeview, along with the city's historic African-American community, have dealt with ongoing frustration as they face the reality of a power structure invested in maintaining itself and seemingly unwilling to allow what it sees as "newcomers"[11] into the circle of power at other than a largely token level. This frustration has sparked multiple, grassroots organizing efforts aimed at ensuring that these communities of color are visible and partly due to that pressure, both the local government and the school district have been involved in a series of policy initiatives attempting to respond to the changing community. However, there has been little change in recent years in terms of significant successes for students of color. A recent report by a local non-profit organization paints a bleak picture of the situation facing African-Americans in Lakeview, including problems with employment and homeownership, health care outcomes and incarceration rates. Similar information released by local Latino organizations notes disparities as well. Many Latino workers who do not have legal documents face harassment at work and are often the victims of wage theft simply because their employers (often Latino themselves) know that the workers feel too vulnerable to complain.

This influx of Latino immigrants – overwhelmingly working-class families from Mexico or families of Mexican descent from south Texas or the US Southwest, as well as a number of Central and South Americans – comes in the context of a small city that is, in terms of power both symbolic and material, overwhelmingly white. A key issue, then, becomes the deceptively simple one of visibility; too often, the Latino population seems to virtually disappear, swallowed up by the restaurant kitchens and long hallways where so many workers spend their days. Their children, however, are fast becoming a substantial and inescapable presence throughout Lakeview's schools.

THE SCHOOL

Prairie Heights High School is located in an upper middle class neighborhood, not far from Lakeview's university. It is one of Lakeview's pricier areas, and the homes are spacious and well cared-

---

[11] Perhaps not surprisingly, White residents who are new to Lakeview do not have to deal with this obstacle.

for. Many families have beautifully maintained gardens and a stroll down a street near Prairie Heights offers evidence that most families are able to spend a fair amount on recreation, as garages and driveways house high-end bicycles and other sporting equipment. The students in the immediate neighborhood come largely from professional, mostly White families. Many of the families have ties to the local university and by the time they get to high school, the students have a clear sense of themselves as competent, and often excellent, students. College is an option many of those students take for granted and many of them will end up in very selective universities or colleges. Their families are generally able to spend considerable   amounts of money on extracurricular activities, including travel, music and other fine arts, and a variety of sports. Other students, however, come from the city's poorer sections, including several low-income apartment complexes that are routinely in the news for drug problems, gun-related incidents and the like. These neighborhoods are less likely to have sidewalks or nearby grocery stores, and the families have far less disposable income to spend on their children. Many new immigrants live in these neighborhoods, which are quite racially mixed and are home to a number of vibrant community centers. When the school buses pull up to Lakeview in the morning and open their doors, most of the kids getting off the bus are students of color. The larger area they come from includes a few neighborhoods which have been an ongoing topic of conversation among Lakeview politicians and community leaders as a "blighted" area and city officials have earmarked monies to several community development projects there over the last decades. In addition to these areas, some of Lakeview's newer suburban areas make up part of the Prairie Heights attendance area, and those students tend to be upper middle class. These neighborhoods are more traditionally suburban, with spacious homes, well-tended lawns and few neighborhood businesses in walking distance.

During my first year in room 134 at Prairie Heights, White students made up 62% of the school's total population. African American students were 14%, Asian student 12% and Latino students 11%.[12] Latino students make up 25% of one of the middle schools that

---

[12] In just a few years, the population has changed. White students are now 55% of the school, Latino students are about 15% and a new

feeds into Prairie Heights, so it seems safe to say that the Latino population at the high school will continue to grow. Prairie Heights routinely publicizes and honors its National Merit Scholars, honor roll students and other students receiving academic accolades. Students also receive much recognition for their involvement in music and arts, though as other scholars have underscored in a similar context, arts is relatively narrowly defined (Lee, 2005). Sports are also popular at the school, with soccer and basketball as the most prestigious sports for both boys and girls. Soccer is particularly competitive at Prairie Heights, but though there are a number of Latino leagues in town and many of the Latino male students are soccer fanatics, very few Latino students play school-affiliated soccer. Students who are on the college-bound track have a variety of advanced courses available, and those students tend to do quite well after high school. In essence, there are two schools within the single school building. The sorting is such that students are segregated by math levels from 9th grade on, with tracking increasing each year.s Certain areas of the school house more of the advanced classes while, special education and ESL are housed side by side. Students who enter and stay in the college-bound track receive an education competitive with an expensive private school. Other students tend to fall through the cracks.

So, when the school or its students are discussed at a public level, it becomes clear that only a certain type (indeed, a numerical minority) of the school's students are understood as an integral part of the school community. The students of color are generally excluded from that community. One school activist noted that the Lakeview school district would be "burned to the ground" if it so ill-served its White students.[13]

THE CLASSROOM

As noted, Lakeview has seen many demographic changes in recent years, changes which have had an enormous impact on Prairie Heights.

---

category – one or more races – is just under 8%. The African American and Asian populations remain the same.

[13]It is important to note that social class of course also plays an important role in how students experience school. That, alas, will have to be the focus of another study.

While research could be carried out in many different areas of the school, I chose to concentrate on one specific classroom – room 134, a Spanish class for native speakers. For one class session a day, the students not only could speak Spanish, they were encouraged to do so—and also to hone their skills in reading and writing Spanish. Cultural, social and political issues that the students would likely not have encountered in other classes came up and provided the context for an academic experience important for its commitment to both educating and empowering the students.

To understand how Latino students are either able or unable to "do" school, I look at their own sense of self as students. As I attempt to unravel and pull clear the many threads that make up the academic and cultural identities of the Spanish speaking immigrant students who are the focus of my study, it is imperative that I deploy a complex and nuanced understanding of those many threads. Immigrant students who come to the US are almost immediately faced with the tremendous racialization that continues to hold sway in US society and, more specifically, in US schools. For that reason, an indispensable lens for my study has been that of Critical Race Theory. This is taken up in a subsequent chapter, but for our purposes now we can understand it to mean that race matters, and that it still has extreme salience in the lives of these students. While "whiteness" and related issues of visibility are important elements in purely descriptive terms, they must also be taken into account in terms of the relevant literature (both theoretical, as well as that which is more rooted in practice) that informs my research.

If Critical Race Theory is to provide much of the essential context, the backdrop against which I conceive my study is the very palpable reality of the US-Mexican border. Through the students' eyes, I have learned to see the border as it exists for them – simultaneously as myth and as reality. As I began my study, I was aware, if only to a degree, of the often crushing reality of the border—as a physical obstacle, more than anything, to the economic and social fortunes of many of the students and families whose stories are at the center of my work. Several months into my study, however, my understanding of the border and its utter centrality to the lives of these students exploded. For those in the US with the papers, and skin color, to ensure that few questions regarding our right to belong will be asked – indeed, we are granted that right as unearned privilege – the border is perhaps most often understood as the 'edge' of something—something far away and not often considered. But for the students and so many in their situation, the border is an invisible, yet oppressive and psychologically powerful line that divides this world they are in from a world they have left behind.

We must ask what it means for these students to be going through high school in the context of an increasingly aggressive backlash against Latino immigrants.[14] Not having legal documentation is decisive not only in how the students are treated, but also in how they see themselves and their future, as this issue of 'belonging' or 'citizenship' plays out on a profoundly psychic level.

I have overheard both student teachers and teachers ask, "Why are *these* students here?" (my emphasis) They are referring to Latino, Hmong and other immigrants they deal with on a daily basis and the not so subtle insinuation is that "they" are somehow "sapping" our resources. Thankfully, this is not the majority stance, but even many who are not overtly hostile to this new wave of immigrants may not be clear about *why* so many immigrants have come here. I argue that this distinction is important because the common wisdom that the United States is such an ideal destination that any and all foreigners would of course want to come here feeds into a colonial mentality that actually underpins the way too many teachers and administrators see their immigrant students. A fundamental lack of understanding about *where* the immigrant students come from leads to scant honoring of their culture and language, an attitude that cuts through and across much of what happens to them in the school setting.

Those who cross borders without the proper documentation bear a double burden of invisibility and illegality. Much of my research focused on listening to the stories of a number of Latino students at Prairie Heights. As I began my research, I understood the place of origin as key, as well as understanding that where the students are now is equally influential. After spending more time with the students, I saw each of them in the middle of a journey. At a remove from the research, I understand the students as being part of a fundamental change in US society, as a struggle continues over how language and

---

[14] Some highly charged words or phrases commonly thrown around, particularly in certain sectors of the national media, include "brown tide", "alien" and "illegal".

cultural markers are repositioned. How the school system understands the changing position of these students (and those who follow) will be critical for the long-term success of these students, as well as for the overall health of a school in the midst of this transformation whose consequences are as yet unknown.

Chapter 1
Untangling Many Threads

Understanding the students in room 132 and their place at Prairie Heights requires a framework that brings together a number of elements, each vital to clearly contextualizing their complicated situation. The extremely complex tangle of issues that serve as a backdrop for the stories of the students whose voices are heard here include the multiple ways in which race and racial politics inform each student's experience at school, as well as the students' status as English language learners and how that is understood by the schools. Also of great relevance is the salience of immigration and legal status (absolutely relevant as so many of the students in my study are undocumented), particularly in an area that has historically had few Latino immigrants, along with the tremendous significance, both material and psychic, of the border itself.

While I began with a series of questions and a clear sense of the many issues involved, I entered room 134 with an equally strong sense of the necessity of listening to the students. The practice of *testimonio* forms the foundation for my study. The tradition of *testimonio* is explicitly linked to the traumatic events of war and violence that ravaged much of Central and Latin America in the 1970s and 80s, and unlike more traditional anthropological or sociological discussions of violence, places the protagonists very explicitly at the center of the stories being told – both in terms of the specifics of the narratives but also, and as importantly, in terms of whose voice is constructed as "expert" and worth listening to. Thus, the protagonists of these stories transcend mere victimhood and become agents of change, as they are powerful transmitters of their own stories (Beverly, 1989, 1993, 2004: Mallon, 2001).

I do not suggest that the experiences of the immigrant students at Prairie Heights are as palpably violent; however, in almost every case, the students I spoke with alluded to the great psychic pain felt by their parents as they made their way to the US, and by themselves, albeit often in markedly different ways, as the younger generation. The tool and practice of *testimonio* offers itself as a way to both analyze and honor the many stories I heard.

A FLUID RACIAL DIVIDE

Understanding the students in room 134 would have been impossible without a close look at the role of race in their lives. Race is a constant and palpable, if always changing, presence in US culture and one whose salience is particularly pronounced in the school setting (Blau, 2003; Darder and Torres, 2004; Gregory, Skiba and Noguera, 2010; Noguera, 2008; Sleeter, 2005; Tatum, 1997). Schools are sites that are highly raced, both replicating and often amplifying some of the racial tensions and realities that exist in the larger community. At school, as well as outside, race works in a number of ways, defining and delimiting access to wealth, opportunity and full inclusion. We have seen how race as a signifier of status and inclusion in the United States has sometimes been fairly fluid. Looking at the history of immigration to the US, we see that some groups, though treated poorly at first, were later allowed in under the expanding umbrella of "whiteness" (Ignatiev, 1995; Painter, 2012). At the same time, racial barriers were often strengthened and enshrined in both policy and behavior (Lipsitz, 1998), and science was frequently invoked as a bludgeon against people of color (Gould, 1996; Painter, 2010; Takaki, 1993). As Cornel West (1994) reminds us, race has tremendous power that is at once symbolic and concrete.

Parallel to the notion of *testimonio*, and absolutely central to my work, is the contextual touchstone and lens provided by Critical Race Theory. Now often used as an explanatory tool in educational research, CRT first came into use in the area of legal studies and, not surprisingly, its birth is linked to concrete political struggles. In this sense as well, it provides a most fitting framework for my work, as I find it necessary to closely link the lived experiences of students in the schools to both the theoretical underpinnings that guide and inform my work, as well as the larger political context. Widely regarded as the founding father of CRT, Bell (1987) begins with a premise that seems both straightforward and fairly simple – that racism is a normalized, ongoing element in US life and therefore permeates the legal system as well.

In the legal context, CRT pushes us to a deeper understanding of the ways in which the legal system actually facilitates racism and inequitable relations of power, a departure from a vision that sees the system itself as pure, and only occasionally tainted by racism and issues of power (Bell, 1980, 1987; Delgado, 1991; Haney López, 2000). Critical Race Theory respects the tradition of storytelling and the insight that narratives can offer in a context of reflective engagement, or the notion of constructing a different social reality through a particular kind of discourse, precisely as we see in the tradition of *testimonio*. Alongside storytelling, CRT articulates the concept of counter-storytelling as a way to reframe common wisdom, "to help us understand when it is time to reallocate power" (Delgado, 2000, p. 61). Solórzano and Yosso (2009) explicate the use of counter-storytelling as an analytical tool for CRT research and warn against the ways that a deficit perspective has often permeated narratives, uncritically and as truth.

Bell touched off an ongoing debate by questioning who was served by the 1954 Brown v. BoE Supreme Court decision mandating desegregation of US schools, contending that the much-lauded decision actually extended further advantages, both political and economic, to many White students, rather than strengthening the educational situation of Black students. Bell notes as well that Whites have historically tended to support policies that lead to advances for Blacks only when those advances also support White interests, a phenomenon he dubbed *interest convergence* (Bell, 1980).[15] Delgado and Stefancic (2000), pioneers in the application of Critical Race Theory, build on this stance, noting that the normative state of affairs in US society, and thus its institutions, is shot through with a racist ideology that serves very specific purposes, and works not only *against* people of color but also very profoundly works *for* white people, despite many protestations to the contrary.

---

[15] This stance is echoed in Lipsitz's (1998) work on what he refers to as 'the possessive investment in whiteness'.

While CRT later expanded beyond legal studies into other fields, including rhetoric and composition, its principal themes have proved to be particularly relevant in the field of education. Ladson-Billings and Tate (1994) were pioneers in understanding not only the applicability of CRT to the field of education, but also its necessity as a theoretical tool. Firmly anchoring their work to key intellectual moorings of African-American scholarship, Ladson-Billings and Tate pay homage to W.E.B. DuBois (1903) and Carter Woodson (1933), and then turn their attention to the ongoing racial issues facing schools today. They argue that race as an explanatory factor is woefully untheorized in educational research, and hold that understanding the weight of race is absolutely essential for a deep understanding of the crushing, and growing, inequalities in our schools today. While their initial work deals primarily with the historically key black-white divide in US schools, it also provides an indispensable framework for deepening our understanding of facial politics in US schools and paves the way for further analysis.

Latino Critical Race Theory, or LatCrit theory, grew out of a deep concern with a fairly rigid conceptualization of race in the US, a simplistic either-or construct, understood as "the conception that race in America consists, either exclusively or primarily, of only two constituent racial groups, the Black and the White" (Perea, 2000, p. 346). Perea took the academy to task for not looking more closely at the extremely complicated and sometimes confusing tapestry of race in the US, and thus perpetuating a simplistic, as well as ahistorical, view of race and race relations in the US. Martinez (1995) and Haney López (1998) offer important insight on how race has been experienced and understood by Latinos and Mexican-Americans in the United States.

Yosso points to the "layers of racialized subordination that make up Chicana/o and Latino/a experiences" (2005, p. 170) as she further questions that Black/White binary. She warns against "some sort of oppression sweepstakes" (Yosso, 2005, p. 170), of key relevance to my understanding of the racial map at Prairie Heights, and highlights the importance of what she calls a transdisciplinary perspective, citing many others who have expanded the scope of CRT by including other perspectives in their respective analyses. Delgado and Stefancic (2001) point to the ongoing importance of storytelling and counter-storytelling in LatCrit theory, and posit that Acuna's (1998) revisioning of the history   of   the   Southwest   from   a   Chicano/Mexican-American perspective demands a new political understanding of the US. That understanding is particularly crucial in the context of schools and the current attempts to strip immigrant students of access to post-secondary education. Solórzano and Delgado Bernal (2001) discuss resistance from a LatCrit perspective, as they consider two key events in Chicano/a student resistance – the East LA high school walkouts in 1968 and the 1993 UCLA student strike demanding a Chicano/a studies program. The ongoing struggle in the Tucson Unified School District to maintain the successful Raza Studies program resonates within this framework as well.[16]

I build on the substantial and complex history of CRT scholarship as I work to understand the ways that race informs the lives of the students in room 134. My stance is interdisciplinary, incorporating a clear historical perspective as part of my LatCrit framework, taking care to ground my gaze in the global south, and recognizing the cultural wealth and experience it can provide us all. The larger political context, including border politics, linguistic capital and the like, provides an indispensable foundation and greatly informs the way in which I look at issues that might sometimes be seen as more exclusively 'language-related' or the exclusive purview of school policy. Yet the older paradigm continues to dominate. These newer students do not fit into the traditional categories of white and black, yet those racial categories continue to play a key role in their school lives. Much of what immigrant students must deal with as they attempt to become part of their new communities is informed by issues of race and racial politics, as they affect both the larger community and the school setting.

While the US-Mexican borders today defines much about the lives of people on both sides, the 'border' as such did not really take legal form until 1924 when the Border Patrol began to operate. The border soon morphed into both beacon and barrier, representing a painful split in a community that did not recognize the harshness of a political border that came to divide once-whole communities.

Haney López (2006) discusses the very explicit ways in which immigration laws, specifically the racial prerequisites to obtaining

---

[16]See the 2011 documentary film, *Precious Knowledge*, which details the struggle in Tucson to continue and strengthen *Raza* Studies.

citizenship, were constructed around a static notion of a White, European nation. The first wave of exclusionary legislation against a particular group came with the Chinese Exclusion Laws in 1882 (Takaki, 1993). As increasing numbers of immigrants came to the US from Southern and Eastern Europe, and many became politically active, Congress passed severely restrictive immigration quota laws in the 1920s as a direct move to limit those immigrants, as well as others from Africa and Asia (Zinn, 2003). It was not until the Great Depression that the full force of US law was turned against Mexican immigrants as well as many who were of Mexican descent but were US-born, and who became the target of increasingly draconian measures, including the round-up and summary deportation of some two million Mexicans during the 1930s (Flores, 2003; Guerin-Gonzalez, 1996; Zinn, 2003). While Mexican immigrants were often openly recruited by large growers and others in need of cheap labor, economic downturns in the US inevitably led to harsh pressure on the immigrant population and, importantly, those who 'looked' like immigrants, whatever their actual legal status happened to be. As we see today with the devastating *redadas*[17] of Mexican and Central American immigrants throughout the upper Midwest and across the US, and the increasing criminalization of immigrants, "looking Mexican" immediately identifies one as *not* belonging; this often means that even those who are legal US citizens may not be able to pass visual muster and thus have to suffer the trauma of deportation or other legal consequences.

Rapid demographic changes in the US in recent decades have affected the academy, of course, and influenced the ways in which scholars think and where they train their gaze. In an analysis of much relevance to the students in room 134, Johnson uses a CRT framework to examine US immigration legislation over history, and calls on CRT schools to carefully analyze "how immigration law operates to exclude non-white racial minorities" (Johnson, 2002, p. 195). While students to date have been included in public schools independent of their legal status[18], the troubled and race-specific history of immigration laws

---

[17] Round-ups, carried out by Immigration and Customs Enforcement (ICE), under the umbrella of the Department of Homeland Security.

[18] The state of Texas in 1975 passed legislation that denied state funds to undocumented K-12 students and allowed local school districts to

helps us to understand that their ongoing status remains that of second-class citizens, both within and outside of the school walls.

Today, we are witness to an increasingly segregated order[19] in the public schools that often affects both the achievement levels and the emotional safety of students (Howard, 2008; Kozol, 1992, 2005). Much of that order is maintained by the strict use of supposedly color-blind rules and regulations that revolve around a school-based notion of citizenship which has at its heart a norm that is fairly simplistic, and ultimately fairly exclusive.[20] Using a somewhat insidious discourse of democratic, 'equal' treatment that obliterates cultural differences and essentializes all students as somehow the same, schools often play the role of exacerbating already existing social inequalities (Blau, 2003; Bonilla-Silva, 2006). Oftentimes, discussions of multiculturalism and diversity are conceived of within a traditionally liberal context in which a white norm is assumed, rather than explicitly articulated, and thus more difficult to understand or, more importantly, resist.[21] Ladson-Billings and Tate argue that "the current multicultural paradigm is mired in liberal ideology that offers no radical change in the current order" (1995, p. 22). In many ways, the discourse (by now, well-practiced, if rarely achieved) in schools around fairness and equity can actually lead to great injustice.[22]

---

bar undocumented students from enrolling. That decision was overturned by the US Supreme Court in its 1982 Plyer v. Doe decision.

[19]I use racialized here in the sense intended by Omi and Winant (1994). In short, a group of people (in this case, students) is seen as little more than their race. This has profound implications for how that group is treated.

[20]Just as US society has historically excluded many people from full voice and citizenship; we see that school structures often replicate that exclusion. While all may attend, students enter the schools doors on very different footing.

[21]I saw this explicitly in the many school events I attended at Prairie Heights; the norm is simply *there*, never up for discussion and understood as static and immune to change.

[22]Though David Gillborn's work looks at the situation in England, his understanding of a "more powerful version of white supremacy; one

Schools often pride themselves, at least at the level of a declared mission, as being communities that are accepting and tolerant of all. This is certainly the case at Prairie Heights, and there are important ways in which that is true. The claim is frequently phrased in language that suggests that all students are, and will be, treated equally. By claiming to treat all students 'equally', rather than treating them equitably[23], schools do not acknowledge the obvious differences in student histories and experiences, and in fact abdicate their responsibility to address and understand those histories and experiences.

The literature on how race is enacted in public schools notes that racial issues often play out to the great academic and emotional disadvantage of students of color whose very selves may be at stake (Blau, 2003; Delpit, 1995; Noguera, 2002). This works on several levels, both in terms of larger societal strictures as well as the more daily relevant institutionalized and embedded racial norms in a given school setting. These norms result in the invisibility of students of color, and underscore the formidable strength of racial fear and resentment on the part of normative figures against the 'other'. An equally important reality for students is how they feel in a given setting, and how they *live* the racially charged reality imposed upon them (Darder, 1995; Suarez-Orozco, 1995; Valdes, 2001).

Feagin and Sikes (1994) pointed to the clear racialization of many public spaces in the US in their work on how the Black middle class is affected daily by the weight of racism. Other scholars offer a clear sense of how racialization in the public arena of schools specifically affects Latino students (Noguera, 2002; Ruiz, 1997). Barajas and Ronnkvist's study (2007) of Chicano/Latino students reveals how those students consistently understood their academic environment as 'White space'. Though they are speaking of college students, their further conceptualization of space as racially ordered is quite relevant for my discussion of Prairie Heights in general and the students in room 134 in

---

that is normalized and taken for granted" (Gillborn, 2009, p. 51) is quite useful in the context of Lakeview and Prairie Heights.

[23]Preservice teachers often insist on "fair" treatment of their students, which often seems to mean a refusal to acknowledge the significant amounts of privilege or obstacles that students may have.

particular. They highlight the strength of the way race works in schools, arguing against a stance that attributes instances of discrimination to individual teachers or staff members, noting that "the organizational logic in schools is racialized and delineates along lines of race" (Barajas and Ronnkvist, 2007, p. 23).

LATINO STUDENTS IN US SCHOOLS

What has been the racial experience of Latino students in the US? A look at those students over the course of the last half century or so presents a disheartening picture (Carter, 1970; Donato, 1997; Gonzalez, 2000; San Miguel, 1987; Trujillo, 1998). Mexicans and Mexican-Americans have long been forced onto the periphery of US society; in fact, one could argue that their educational fate in the US mirrors the way in which the US has treated Mexico and indeed, the entire region of Central and Latin America, in its ongoing inequitable political and economic dealings with that region.

In his work on Mexican-Americans and schooling, Carter (1970) describes a history of 'educational neglect' in which students were seen as coming from a somehow deficient culture and many were sent into remedial programs they never left (Donato, 1997). A number of schools worked to make their Mexican students into "facsimiles of middle-class children" (Carter, 1970, p. 35). San Miguel (1997) notes many rural Mexican-Americans in Texas simply didn't attend school in the early decades of the 20th century. They were agricultural laborers and oftentimes, family financial need meant there was not a huge incentive to send the children to school. As was the case with many so-called minority groups, Mexican students were trained (a more apt word in this context than educated) primarily to become workers on the lowest rungs of the economic ladder.[24] Sánchez (1997) writes about the so-called Mexican schools and the longstanding, *de facto*, segregation of Mexican students in the Southwest, Texas and California. The situation was successfully challenged in Los Angeles

---

[24]Takaki discusses the language used by school officials to talk about *Mexican* children, a term those educators used loosely to refer to both Mexicans and Mexican Americans, unmindful of language and cultural differences. He quotes one school official as saying, "we don't need skilled or white-collared Mexicans" (Takaki, 1998: 156).

in the 1920s, when the Mexican consulate in Los Angeles worked together with a group of Mexican-American leaders to form *La Escuela México*, a school that taught in both Spanish and English and worked hard to preserve Mexican traditions and culture (Sánchez, 1993).

Native Spanish-speaking students chafed under draconian language policies, including the submersion of non-English speaking students into all-English environments. Not surprisingly, studying in such environments with virtually no formal instruction in English made it very difficult for many students to make significant academic progress, and forced them to pick up English in a largely conversational, rather than formal, manner. At the same time, it left them "floating in a sea of Anglo conformity" (Stein, 1986, p. 8). Huge numbers of Mexican students were unable to make it in this context, and ended up slipping far behind their grade levels, and many dropped out. Those who stayed were saddled with the label of "culturally deprived' children, often facing punishment merely for speaking Spanish (Griego-Jones, 2001). This sparked much ongoing, if often somewhat subterranean, resistance among students and families, with a notable case the Chicano high school students and activists in the late 1960s who pushed the Los Angeles school board to allow students to speak Spanish, and to offer some instruction relevant to the students' needs and cultural backgrounds.[25]

While many people in the US have a notion, albeit cursory, of the historical black-white divide in US education, the ways in which Mexican and Mexican-American students were similarly segregated and offered fewer opportunities are rarely discussed.[26]   Mexican and

---

[25] Thousands of high school students in East Los Angeles organized massive walkouts (also known as 'blowouts'), with more than 20,000 students, in the spring of 1968 to protest school policies that prohibited students from speaking Spanish, channeled most students into a vocational track and refused to teach students about Mexican or Chicano history (2008 *Democracy Now* interview with Moctesuma Esparza, one of the organizers of the walkouts and producer of a film dramatizing those events). See also Solórzano and Delgado Bernal (2001).

[26] This parallels the fact that Mexican history is rarely taught in the US, a fact commented on by several students in room 134.

Mexican-American students were frequently segregated into under-financed "Mexican schools" and, in fact, their struggles for more equitable educational opportunities were part of the demands that paved the way for the 1954 Brown v. BoE desegregation decision (Portales, 2000). The 1946 Mendez v. Westminster decision was a class action suit challenging school segregation and representing some 5,000 Mexican American students in California (Valencia, 2005). A district court eventually ruled that the students' rights had indeed been violated, but the case never went all the way to the US Supreme Court.

Montejano (1987) has discussed the "racing" of Mexican immigrant students upon their arrival in Texas, while Acuña (1998) argues that Mexican immigration has historically been linked to a palpable sense of both fear and contempt of the 'other', a point also made by de León (1983). While race is a potent social variable in most Latin American countries, it plays out somewhat differently in the US. Once in the US, immigrant students must deal with what may be a change in both class and racial status. What is considered *blanco* and accorded status in a given Latin American country may translate into not white enough once the border is crossed.[27]

A New Landscape

During the 1980s, a new group of Latino immigrants began to arrive in the US. As a direct result of US policy in the region, Salvadorans and Nicaraguans started to arrive, fleeing the political and military crises in their countries. Many Salvadorans, Guatemalans and Nicaraguans left for overtly political reasons in the early 1980s, though only the Nicaraguans were routinely granted political asylum.[28] Also during the 1980s, the economic devastation in the region led to a large exodus

---

[27] The stories of many immigrants to the Lakeview district bear this out. Mexican and Central American immigrants who enjoyed a slight social edge in their countries because of their lighter skin color were more surprised to encounter racism, both overt and subtle, in the US than were the darker immigrants I spoke to.

[28] As the US supported the military governments in El Salvador and Guatemala, it was difficult for citizens of those countries to gain legal entry to the US.

from Mexico, following a huge devaluation of the *peso* (Massey, 1997). By the late 1980s, however, the economic crisis in Central America, related to the US-financed military activities there, led to tens of thousands of people heading to the US for economic reasons. Additionally, more immigrants began to arrive in the US from Honduras[29] and Panama, while the number from Costa Rica remained minimal (Portes and Rumbaut, 2001). The young immigrants who came as K-12 students changed the dynamic in a number of public school districts, most notably Los Angeles, Washington, D.C., and Miami (Suárez-Orozco, 1989). And, while Mexican immigrants have long been a significant population in both schools and society in the Southwest, in Texas and California for the last 15 years or so, they have also begun to make an impact on a number of smaller school districts in areas that historically were fairly homogenous, including many cities and towns across the upper Midwest (Crowley, Lichter and Qian, 2006; Vargas, 2002).

The new waves of immigration touched off a still-simmering polemic regarding language policy. Immigrants who spoke languages other than English as their first language demanded appropriate educational opportunities, sparking a political backlash among some politicians and policy makers, one that resonated precisely among the children and grandchildren of many of those European immigrants who had constructed an idealized past, in which all immigrants somehow magically learned English with little trouble. This led to a number of initiatives to impose English-only legislation, with the oft-cited argument that earlier (read: European) groups of immigrants quickly learned English; the assumption became that today's immigrants do not *want* to learn English. This is debatable at best, as many early immigrants often lived and worked in virtual linguistic enclaves and in fact, many of them were effectively marginalized from real power or status (Salmons and Wilkerson, 2008). Many students dropped off the educational map early, entered the workforce, and were not much of a concern for school or other public authorities. Nonetheless, they fed and continue to feed the US success narrative, one that is racially skewed, because they were able, by and large, to become economically

---

[29]There is a small but significant number of Hondurans in and around Lakeview.

successful and stable in a relatively short period of time.[30]   This experience thus becomes a bludgeon against what current immigrants, overwhelmingly people of color, experience.

Today, the single largest and ongoing group of immigrants in the public schools comes from Mexico (Portes and Rumbaut, 2001; US Census data). During the 1980s and early 1990s, many Mexicans entered the US to work, often returning to family commitments on a cyclical basis (Appleby, Moreno and Smith, 2009; Escárcega and Varese, 2004).[31] Mexican immigration to the United States increased dramatically after the enactment of the North American Free Trade Agreement (NAFTA) in 1994 that sent many small farmers and merchants across Mexico into bankruptcy as they were unable to compete with the sweeping economic measures that devastated the peasant economy and small businesses, with Mexico flooded by an influx of US goods, including foodstuffs, against which the average farmer or merchant could not compete (Gonzalez, 2000). In large measure, these immigrants had far less formal education than their counterparts of the early 1980s from the wave of immigration which followed the *peso* devaluation and carried many college-educated professionals in its wake (Perez and Salazar, 1997; Portes and Rumbaut, 2001).

While immigration is a sociological phenomenon, and the history of human movement across the US-Mexican border is both complicated and intricate, the US response to the stepped-up immigration has been largely punitive. Rather than attempting to deal with the internal conditions, to no small extent directly linked to US policies, that have sparked increasing numbers of people to attempt to find their fortunes across the border, the US has responded by pouring money into Immigration and Customs Enforcement, militarizing huge sections of the US-Mexican border and often harassing activists who seek to help

---

[30] Not insignificantly, entering the workforce as a factory worker in one's teens often led to life-long employment. Union jobs paid well enough that a worker could afford a home and support a family. That is simply no longer possible.

[31] The cyclical comings and goings were quite common even in the Lakeview school district until the border became much more difficult and dangerous to cross.

the immigrants entering the United States (Hayduk, 2009).   The militarization of the border is without precedent and has significantly changed the way many immigrant families live (Durand and Massey, 2004).

Whether or not one speaks English can translate into particular positions in shifting hierarchies within groups of Latinos. Those who are recently arrived may disparage what they see as others' too-quick embrace of English and US culture. Legal status creates its own unique tensions. While many in the Latino community are in active solidarity with the undocumented workers in this country, others are not. According to CNN exit polls, one-fourth of Latino voters were in favor of California's Proposition 187, the so-called Save our State legislation that prohibited both state and local governments from providing a broad range of services to undocumented immigrants.   However, support of immigrants cuts across traditional party lines and the growing public voices of Latinos—advocacy groups like LULAC and MALDEF, as well as more mainstream presences like Univision, the Spanish-language TV channel based in New York City, and a whole array of Spanish-language radio stations in markets like Los Angeles, New York and other major urban areas--are overwhelmingly in support of immigrants and immigrant rights (Felix, González and Ramírez, 2008; Po, 1998).

SPEAKING IDENTITY

Another vital thread of this study is understanding the significance of language for the students at Prairie Heights.   At the heart of one's identity, language marks us, identifies us and creates the spaces in which we act and interact. Thus, not surprisingly, many of the school-based programs dealing with language are also, if not always explicitly, about culture as well.   Underpinning much of school lives is an ongoing process of socialization. With immigrant students, it is often hard to separate socialization from "Americanization". This process of Americanization skews along racial lines and therefore is often aimed at US-born students, who may be African- American, Chicano, Hmong but are not seen as having properly absorbed US (understood as white, middle-class) school culture (Schmidt, 2000).   Laurie Olsen, in her study of a California high school points out that "to be American is to be English-speaking, white-skinned and Christian" (Olsen, 1997, p. 55)

The students in my study are native Spanish speakers, and in many educational contexts they might be understood primarily, if not exclusively, in terms of their linguistic identity--often only as students who have yet to "master" English. Each of these students also embodies an identity that is seen as "other" in the context of the school they attend, and strongly identifies as "Latino" or "Mexican," sometimes both, in contrast to the overwhelming majority of students in the school. The students intuit, and sometimes even enforce, a somewhat racialized hierarchy among themselves.[32] But this was rarely understood or recognized by the larger school community and once they left room 134, they were an undifferentiated body in the eyes of the school. As the culture is not taken seriously, oftentimes we see a situation in which the Spanish language itself becomes identified with second-class status. Thus the valuable wealth of incoming immigrant students is largely ignored. While Spanish in the context of Lakeview has taken on the patina, to a certain degree, of a language of the working poor in this city, there are nevertheless many in the community who would like their children to learn Spanish, for reasons ranging from purely pragmatic to those who embrace different cultures and languages.

A hierarchy of languages is still at play, even when we are speaking exclusively of Spanish, as is perhaps best expressed in the fact that for years only Castilian Spanish was taught in high schools, even though the Spanish which students were likely to encounter outside of class would have been from Latin America. Clearly, some languages have more symbolic power than others, as some are more "recognized" than others. Identity becomes perhaps an even more critical issue in a context such as Lakeview, when the presence, either material or symbolic, of a wide range of role models is relatively scarce. There is no *barrio*, per se, in Lakeview and there are few public gathering spaces for the Latino population. What does it mean for an immigrant student to learn English in a context where his/her native language is rarely celebrated and not always even recognized as legitimate? Of

---

[32] This sorting out was not based exclusively on race, though that did play into the way students saw each other; the whitest students were seen as less "authentic", and that took on more weight if the student was not from Mexico, and had legal documentation to be in the US.

course, when Spanish is a language mastered by honor students, it becomes a legitimate endeavor. But the Spanish of the native Spanish speakers, ironically, is largely ignored and often looked down upon in the larger school community. Offering both an overview and a brief history of some of the shifts in language policy in the United States over the last several decades or so, Schmidt (2000) points to the common mode of "English immersion" or total immersion in a 'sink or swim' methodology. Ironically, many of those immigrants affected by this policy and their children have so revised the narrative of immigration that they are among the most ardent defenders of what is a pedagogically tenuous method at best. In any case, many of the students subjected to this method simply did not make it in academic terms. In today's context, where academic excellence is expected by the schools, or at least promised to the parents of most public school children, this pedagogical method has come into increasing conflict.

Schmidt (2000) describes both how earlier generations of English language learners essentially lost their languages as well as the fact that the huge upsurge in immigration after the 1950s forced the issue of bilingual education in a number of US school districts. Minami and Ovando (1995) discuss the rapid influx of immigrants from Asia and Latin America in the 1980s, noting that language minority students are the fastest-growing group in US schools, a trend that continues today. Also important for our purposes is the fact that Spanish-speaking households are the fastest-growing sector among language-minority groups in the US. This has been the experience in Lakeview as well.

School-based discourse often ends up being something of a code and there is no official instruction in the language, which is, after all, the language of academic success. Children of a certain class, race and culture come to school with this language already largely mastered, while others struggle for years simply to understand it and, at the same time, see their own strengths and cultural reserves ignored or derided. Those who don't 'get it' are more likely to experience academic failure, with all the accompanying economic consequences.

Jim Cummins, a veteran of the so-called language wars of the late 20th century, attacked the premise, one still held by many educators today, that the "lack of English proficiency is the major reason for language minority students' academic failure" (Cummins, 1981, p. 4). Social and cultural factors are all too often overlooked when achievement is considered (Cummins, 1981; Krashen, 1981) and programs that deal with the lack of English proficiency are generally conceived in terms that are almost exclusively linguistic, rather than cultural or political.

While the common wisdom in many schools understands the ESL curriculum as somehow benign and exclusively linguistic, a number of language researchers (Au, 1993; Moran & Hakuta, 1995; Wong Fillmore, 1991) strongly contested that, arguing that ESL instruction may actually end up marginalizing second language students. Though the ESL curriculum has been used to isolate non-English speaking students and may end up holding them back, critical educators of English language learners are able to confront the old paradigms (Ballenger, 1999; Valdes, 2001). Valenzuela (1999) makes a crucial point, taking on what she calls "subtractive bilingualism", and arguing that most ESL instruction ends up culturally tracking students according to cultural, nonacademic criteria in ways which have profound effects on their academic potential. Because ELL students are considered to be academically deficient, there are generally no advanced courses available to them. Schooling then becomes a "subtractive" process, as the possibility of full and authentic bilingualism and biculturalism is squashed by the programs and policies implemented in many public schools. Students often have fairly fluent social language skills in both English and Spanish, but often cannot write at or even near grade level in either Spanish or English. They thus become functionally illiterate in two languages[33], in what was initially referred to as 'semi-lingualism' (Cummins, 1979). However, linked as it was to a deficit perspective, that term is no longer in favor.[34] Valenzuela (1999), Skuttnab-Kangas (1981) and Pérez and Torres-Guzmán (2002) work from the premise that, in order to

---

[33] I saw this situation many times with my high school students in Nicaragua, many of whom had spent years in ESL programs in Miami. They were unable to write coherently in either English or Spanish.

[34] Cummins (2000) no longer uses the term, though he points out that his intention was always to underscore the problems that potentially bilingual students faced because of language policy and pedagogy, rather than to frame those students as somehow lacking in linguistic or cognitive ability.

authentically and satisfactorily acquire a second language, a student must first master his or her first language.[35]

This subtractive process ultimately leads to disaffection and alienation, perhaps most dangerously even from themselves as students, on the part of Mexican- American students whose school experiences rob them of their natural energy and self-esteem, in an ongoing process of "social decapitalization" (Valenzuela, 1999, p. 261). All too often, the school culture simply does not respond to the daily, lived experiences of English Language Learners and makes it very difficult for them to successfully integrate into the academic world.[36] Immigrant students are regarded as 'limited English proficient' rather than as fluent in Spanish or potentially bilingual.[37] Students absorb these messages and may ultimately end up trying to totally assimilate, which has its own dangers, or, however subconsciously, buying into the belief that they and their communities are not as valuable (García, 2001). As we will see in subsequent chapters, this kind of conflictive relationship with language plays out in the context of Prairie Heights, where the degree to which one speaks English can impact status within groups of Latino students. In what we might understand as resistance to an overwhelmingly new linguistic and cultural reality, those who are

---

[35] The Lakeview district had implemented a number of bilingual programs that were relatively new during the time I carried out my research at Prairie Heights. Since then, they have piloted several dual immersion programs. The dual immersion program, as currently conceived of, work from the understanding that children should learn to read and write in their native language before transitioning to English instruction.

[36] While other students are also undoubtedly poorly served by traditional school culture, my concern in this study is the Latino student population.

[37] A principal at an elementary school in Lakeview with a very high number (over 20%) of native Spanish speakers noted at a public meeting that those students are "all gifted and talented" and lamented the fact that their language skills are rarely fully recognized.

recently arrived sometimes disparage what they see as others' too-quick embrace of English and US culture.[38]

Other scholars (Gutiérrez, Asato, Santos and Gotanda, 2002) have located the ongoing debates about language policy in the more current, heavily politicized context.   Coining the term 'backlash pedagogy', Gutiérrez explains this pedagogical stance as "an institutionalized and political response to the demographic shifts that can no longer be ignored" (Gutiérrez, 2001, p. 566).   In fact, Mexican immigration has historically been linked to a palpable sense of both fear and contempt of the 'other' (Acuña, 1998; Limón, 1998), and that sense continues to be latent in much of the national and local discussions about both immigration and English language policy. Given the above, the actual enacting of such policies in the schools is an essential element to understanding much of what happens to Latino students in those school settings where they are a relatively new population.

THE BORDER AND BELONGING

While race is one of the most salient factors in terms of how students are seen by school authorities, and often how they see themselves, my analysis also weaves in the significance of the border; in other words, the powerful psychic and legal intersection of race with the weight of the border.   As it exists today, a legal crossing of the border provides citizenship, in very real and consequential ways. Many who cross the border without documentation do so at immense personal risk and are forced to live on the margins of society.

My initial concern about the low levels of achievement among Latino students and an ever-growing store of anecdotal evidence convinced me that more attention must be paid to these very specific students in this particular geographical location. While I understood, to a degree, the often crushing reality of the border as a physical obstacle, more than anything, to the economic and social fortunes of many of the students and families whose stories are at the center of my work, my understanding of the border and its utter centrality to the lives of these

---

[38] At Prairie Heights, it was clear that students were facing pressure both to learn English as fast as possible and thus fit in more quickly, while at the same time learning English too quickly left them open to accusations of 'selling out'.

students exploded, so to speak, after some time in room 134. A useful first question is – what is useful to ask what is the border?   Limón's (1998) compelling work on the border regions between Mexico and the United States describes an area he calls "Greater Mexico".   This "place" has long since transcended the physical borders of the greater southwestern region of the United States, and I argue that "Greater Mexico" can be found in many schools and public spaces throughout the US.

An enormous, increasingly militarized land border separates Mexico from the US and it is probably not lost on most Mexicans that the entire US Southwest, as well as California and Texas, were once part of Mexico, making the 'border' crossing bizarre in more than one way. That border and its very fluidity, both much more porous and at the same time more rigid than the air routes that separate the Caribbean islands from Miami or New York, informs both the symbolic and concrete identity not only of the Mexican immigrants who make that crossing, but also of the *gringos* on this side of the border who are often unaware of the tremendously important role that Mexico has played and continues to play in US culture.

Duarte-Herrera works with a "definition of the border as a hyperreality constituted by speeches, practices and experiences of the different social actors" (Duarte-Herrera, 2001, p. 139). While Duarte-Herrera and others (Garcia, 2001; Kearney, 1995) understand the metaphorical and symbolic weight and life of the border, they also see it as continually shaped by the transnational reality of movement of both goods and people, that creates networks and a sort of hyperspace, produced and dramatically affected by "the pervasive globalization of capital" (Duarte-Herrera, 2001, p. 49).   Lugo evokes Foucault and prompts us to "reimagine border theory in the realm of the inescapable, mountainous terrains of power" (Lugo, 2005, p. 44), and that is where my interest lies – in understanding this contested and contentious terrain that extends far beyond those geographic regions that are near the physical US-Mexican border.   I use the term 'the borderlands' (Anzaldúa, 1987) to help understand the space created by students like those in room 134 who are shaped and constricted by its ongoing, material reality, although they are quite distant from the physical border itself.

For those in the United States with the papers and skin color to ensure that few questions regarding our right to belong will be asked –

indeed, we are granted that right as unearned privilege – the border is perhaps most often understood as the 'edge' of something, the periphery. But for the students, the border is an invisible, yet oppressive and psychologically powerful line that divides this world they are in from a world they have left behind, if only temporarily.[39]

ENTERING THE FOLD

For years, US schools have carried out an "Americanizing" function, and they continue to do so today. That aggressive assimilationism is often lauded as it is seen as 'integrating' students into schools, but at what cost? Does it not instead often work to strengthen an internal hierarchy, with some students identified as "more American" than others and thus more entitled to what the school has to offer? As they begin to negotiate the school system after they arrive in the US, immigrant students often face serious conflicts about whether or not, and how, to keep their linguistic and cultural identities intact. Many scholars, including Olsen (1997) and Lee (2005) have pointed out that academic success, both for immigrant students as well as for students who have been constructed as the 'other,' generally because of race, is often linked to how successfully students are able to assume an identity as 'American.'

The notion of citizenship that informs our schools is often hidden and yet profoundly affects student experience, achievement and identity. How is citizenship, a concept that is at once inclusive and exclusive, defined in the public school setting? What are the specific ways in which certain students find themselves outside the framework of citizenship? Students are subjected to many sorting mechanisms, including the obvious ones of academic tracking, alongside the sometimes more subtle mechanisms that throw up barriers which may not be visible or recognized, but whose weight is nonetheless central in defining a student's educational possibilities. These ultimately function to grant, or deny, what I consider full citizenship in the school community.

---

[39] In recent years, many students have taken great risks by openly challenging laws denying them full access to higher education and thus risking arrest and/or deportation. The informal 'undocumented, unafraid and unapologetic' movement highlights these risks.

Yuval-Davis (1997) looks at citizenship as describing the relationship between a particular individual and the state. By substituting "school" for "state," we can begin to hammer out a working definition for use in the school context, including an understanding of the ways in which the concept of citizenship has been applied very differentially to different people. The question of citizenship is further complicated in the school setting, with many schools acknowledging the existence of 'different' groupings, by race or religion, for example, but clearly locating those 'different' groups at a measurable disadvantage vis-à-vis the so-called normative group that defines and regulates school culture. Any discussion of language issues in schools today should take into consideration the sometimes more subterranean concerns of citizenship and belonging, including the ways in which standard language, legal status and other elements form part of a constellation of official 'norms' that serve exclusionary purposes, working to marginalize, rather than authentically integrate, students into a given school community. Ngai's work on different immigrant groups in the US (2004) and the impact that race and class have on those groups and their integration into US society is very instructive for anyone looking at the intertwined issues of immigration and citizenship in an educational setting.

A full understanding of citizenship would include the ways in which students are included in a school culture, on their own terms. Parallel to that is the question of how a student's home culture is understood or legitimized. All too often, students' home cultures are marginalized or even completely 'disappeared.' Because the home culture is so often not seen as legitimate or academic, it is disregarded and, in fact, attempts may be made to replace it. Moll (1992) and Valdes (1996) have written persuasively about the need to incorporate family and community 'funds of knowledge' into school life.

WHO IS LET IN?

For too many students "becoming 'American' means giving up something else. Much literature on the experience of Chicano and Latino students in US public schools speaks to the ways in which, historically, many of these students have overtly resisted attempts to be molded into 'real Americans, 'precisely because of the way in which that label is rigidly defined (Donato, 1997; Hernández-Truyol, 1998;

Valdes, 2001). Olsen's (1997) work on immigrant students in a California school and Lee's (2002) research on Hmong students in a small Midwestern city underscore the way in which "American" is a highly racialized term, as these students clearly understand being "American" as equivalent to being white.[40] Olsen (1997) asks whether schools will be able to fulfill a democratizing function, or if they will simply end up reproducing the existing class, racial and language relations. She identifies schools as one of the few places where established residents and new immigrants are thrown together on a daily basis, and thus a decisive point in that complicated "negotiation of racial and cultural relations" (Olsen, 1997, p. 16). Olsen chronicles a year at an unnamed high school in California, where the demographic changes have been massive, and where a political backlash against the growing immigrant population led to a number of policy changes that have painted many schools into a difficult pedagogical corner.

What is understood as "American" by immigrant students changes fairly quickly, with race being a central factor that students pick up on almost immediately (Olsen, 1997; Suarez-Orozco, 1998; Suarez-Orozco, Suarez-Orozco and Todorova, 2008; Trueba, 1998). Significantly, Olsen also points out that the white students do not even locate their immigrant peers on their maps of the school community. In the context of the Lakeview district, it is clear that while nationality and language are important, race is the pivotal factor at play.

WHITENESS/INVISIBILITY

Though race is at least on the agenda in the public schools, if often in rather cloaked ways, whiteness and white privilege are rarely discussed. Yet an understanding of how whiteness functions as a system of sorting and of immense privilege in the individual lives and practices of teachers, and also at an institutional level, is absolutely fundamental to ensuring any real sense of what goes on in public schools (Fine, Weis, Powell and Wong, 1997; Lipsitz, 1998). Whiteness is systemic, yet is experienced in very personal ways by both students and teachers.

---

[40] Immigrant Latino students at a local high school referred to their white peers as *"los americanos,"* while the African American students were *"los negros,"* and the Hmong students became *"los chinos."*

Hurtado and Stewart (1997) urge us to be conscious about the very use of the term 'whiteness' and to constantly interrogate our notions of whiteness. They note the way in which whiteness is understood as a '"natural" state of affairs," and add that national identity in the US has been constructed as white[41], which we can clearly say happens at the level of school-based identity as well. Kailin notes that teachers who are mostly White and have grown up and been educated in racially and culturally homogenous communities, have a difficult time dealing with rapidly changing demographics in their school districts, living as they do "in a symbolic universe that is 'white' (Kailin, 1996, p. 745). Additionally, as Obidah and Teel (2001) and Ulluci and Battey (2011) have pointed out, White teachers often carry racist (if unconscious) assumptions about their students.[42]

Ladson-Billings' work on African-American students and their teachers (1995; 2000; 2005) has great relevance for Latino students. She notes that much has been made of poor achievement among African American students and posits that those students are seen as somehow "aberrant" and that teachers "presume that (their) job is to rid African American students of any vestiges of their own culture" (Ladson-Billings, 2000, p. 206). Ladson-Billings' position finds resonance in the work of many scholars who are focused more exclusively on the Latino community, and are similarly concerned with issues of culture. Speaking more specifically to the case of Latino students, and directly addressing the issue of lowered expectations, Hernández-Sheets (1995) discusses her experience with what she calls "alternate pedagogy" in a classroom of Mexican and Mexican-American students who were categorized as 'remedial.' Her high expectations of these students led to nearly all of them doing quite advanced work. Students of color, and their parents, will often hear a sort of back-handed praise for receiving mediocre grades; the implication is that "these" students can do no better. They are too often

---

[41] Martinez (1997) offers important historical perspective on Mexican Americans and the construction of Mexicans as "white", even as they experienced significant discrimination and exclusion.

[42] This is true at Prairie Heights as well, and is not a case of individual intent or malice on the part of individual teachers, but rather a highly embedded set of attitudes that shape the school.

steered away from difficult courses, as Hernández-Sheets' students were, under the guise of concern for their self-esteem.[43]   Díaz and Flores (2001) attack the remedial model that has long been applied, often unthinkingly, to Latino students. They cite their own literacy research that showed that teacher willingness to "teach to the potential" of each child, abandoning all deficit beliefs and myths about the child, and, instead, teaching with the premise that each child can succeed, will in fact lead to quite measurable gains. Darder (1995) highlights the role of committed and critical Latino educators in the lives of Latino students. One Lakeview middle school teacher talked about the lack of knowledge that many teachers have. "I know a fair amount about Mexico," she says. "I read a lot, and I'm interested, but I don't really have a clear understanding of the regional and cultural differences within Mexico or how that might play out in a community like Lakeview."

Much of the literature looking specifically at Latino students is based on case studies of student populations in the Southwest or in other areas such as California or large urban areas on the East Coast with historically large populations of Spanish-speaking populations. While those numbers have not always resulted in political power, one could argue that they do afford those populations a certain level of visibility. Even as the Latino population increases in the Lakeview school district and the city itself[44], much of the Latino community continues to be virtually invisible as a presence to the larger community. Teachers in this district need to be even more prepared to see this group as more than just a deficit population, or a cultural oddity.

---

[43] I came up against this quite personally when my son started 6th grade. Having him placed in advanced mathematics was a battle, as the learning coordinator told me how she didn't want to "upset him," or "set him up for failure."

[44] Latino students were nearly 19% of Lakeview students for the 2012-2013 academic year; and the 2010 census put Latinos at just over 6% of the population in Lakeview.

TRACKED INTO FAILURE

Academic tracking is a serious issue in most schools throughout the country, and often begins as early as elementary school. It shapes opportunity, blocking students at an early age from access to traditional academic success, and has a particular impact on the post-secondary years. Much attention has focused on promoting reading at an early age, and elementary schools are likely to have a number of reading programs in place for the K-2 population. While early literacy is certainly fundamental, mastery of mathematics is becoming an equally vital gatekeeper, and can have a profound impact on students' career or educational opportunities. Thus, student progress in mathematics at the middle school level has taken on real importance. Moses and Cobb (2001) call math literacy nothing less than a civil rights struggle, and point out that math illiteracy affects blacks and other minorities more intensely than white students. While many sorting mechanisms were in play, it was quite clear in Prairie Heights that mathematics tracking continues to be one of the most aggressive ways in which students are tracked. Most of the students in room 134 were far behind even the minimum grade standards in mathematics, effectively cutting them off from many post-secondary options. Most of the students were not in one of the several college-bound math tracks, and those who did go on to college had to make up for the math they missed in high school.[45]

Tate (1995) calls for an "Afrocentric" framework in mathematics education that will teach mathematics to students in a language, and within a cultural framework, that is more familiar to them. This approach could well be transferred to Mexican immigrant students, drawing on the considerable cultural wealth of the Mayan and Aztecan cultures, and some of their deep knowledge of mathematics, to teach mathematics in a more culturally appropriate way (Hirsch-Dubin, 2006). Whether or not this happens, one minimal step would be to ensure that students are, at the very least, given mathematics instruction in their own language. Frequently used in the Lakeview middle schools, text-heavy math curricula puts an additional burden on ELLs

---

[45] "It sucks", Adela told me, "I could have done this, I *should* have been doing this in high school", as she described the time spent in remedial math classes.

as they have to first deal with the English before they can "get" to the math .

There are other ways to derail students from the more academically advanced tracks. Many students of color are tagged as having some kind of learning or behavioral disability, and, quite early on in their school career, can end up warehoused into special education classes. At the same time, few students of color are understood as 'talented and gifted', and thus may miss out on extra attention or opportunities that instead go to children who often come from families that are more experienced at negotiating the system.[46]

As we look at the generally grim record of Latino student achievement, we also carefully examine how resistance emerges. There are many ways in which students are able to mobilize against the stifling norms of school culture, even though this may sometimes contradict their own interests. I draw on the Gramscian notion of 'common sense,' as used by Hall (1997) in his effort to make Gramsci available to a new generation of political activists as well as the way it is explicated and deepened in Apple's (1993, 2001) work: that is, we must recognize the logic inherent to the decisions made and actions taken by groups of people, even when those decisions or actions may seem to be detrimental to their long-term interests.

People are not simple dupes of a system, and stripping them of agency or intelligence does little to enhance our understanding of them and their motives. My observations in the field and ongoing conversations with other educators and parents help to shed light on the issues at hand. Parallel to student resistance is the agency of progressive teachers who are able to contribute to a praxis of resistance, sometimes against great odds. Many teachers at Prairie Heights are nothing short of heroic in their ongoing efforts to move beyond an increasingly rigid framework, defined by budget cuts and stepped-up testing, working to really connect with their students. Cho and Apple (1998) look at particular forms of resistance, subjectivity and identity. Like Willis (1977), they discuss students who do things that may not seem rational. Returning agency to these students, they argue that the students choose to do so "in order to live in, transform, or even gain

---

[46]In her study of immigrant students who often function as interpreters, Guadalupe Valdes (2003) urges us to broaden our notion of "gifted".

control over the unfavorable social conditions of their existence" (Cho and Apple, 1998, p. 288). This work helped me to better "see" my students and the logic of what, at first glance, appear to be illogical decisions. For instance, a number of girls in room 134 ended up pregnant, and Latino boys at Prairie Heights often dropped out of school. While the consequences are difficult in both instances, there is an inherent rationality and logic to the students' actions.

Chapter 2

Room 134 and the Shadowlands

My understanding of *testimonio* and my commitment to understanding one piece of the immigrant story sparked and guided my work. As noted in the introduction, a key concern prompting this study was the poor graduation rate posted by Latino students. I made contact with Ms. Lawrence[47], the teacher in room 134, through a connection to Prairie Heights and because I knew that she was teaching a course for native Spanish speakers at the school. I had a fairly good sense of the many issues facing Latino students in the Lakeview district in general, as well as a good 'read' on the specifics of the students at Prairie Heights.

My own position in this story is multiple. While I am a researcher, and committed to understanding in complex and useful ways the keys to either academic success or failure for Latino students, my interest in the Latino population in the schools is also highly personal. My husband is Central American and our children grew up in Central America, where their "double identity" was not particularly remarkable or worthy of comment. They both attended public schools similar to Prairie Heights and their experiences forced me to think critically and seriously about race in ways that I was long allowed to sidestep, as a white woman. I simply no longer have the luxury that many of the teachers and parents have, when they continue to insist to me that "everything's fine." Additionally, having lived abroad for many years, I have been an outsider, albeit one in a position of considerable power. That position affords me a certain understanding which facilitated my research. At the same time, I am mindful of what Gotanda (2003) has

---

[47]None of the names used in this study are real.

called "white innocence" and have worked to respond to Gutiérrez' (2005) challenges to researchers based on Gotanda's work.

I did have a certain 'insider' status for several reasons, with a primary factor being that a number of the male students knew my son from soccer. This helped in terms of them taking me seriously and accepting my respect for them. The fact that I am the mother to two biracial and bilingual sons meant that the students saw me in a slightly different way than they might have had I been 'just' another white woman, and I believe that most of them assumed that I would "get" them. Ms. Lawrence, who was extremely well-liked by the students, mentioned this to me on several occasions as a concrete advantage I had as a researcher, and said that she thought that the boys particularly saw me as being "on their side." Having lived and worked in Nicaragua turned out to be decisive, as the students in room 134 felt that Nicaraguan Spanish was acceptable. They did not feel that way about Spanish from Spain or some of the countries in Latin America (specifically, Argentina, Uruguay and Chile), and that certainly worsened the clear schism between the majority of the students and the one student who came from the Southern Cone. We frequently talked about the way Nahuatl (the Aztec-Toltec language) had significantly influenced language in a huge swath of Mexico and what is today Central America, including Nicaragua. Another link was the fact that I knew a fair amount about the traditional, everyday Mexican foods that are also common in Nicaragua, and was aware of some cultural touchstones that were part of the students' shared culture, if not daily lives. These included the importance of *telenovelas*, or televised soap operas, to popular culture in Mexico; the tremendous attention paid to the Mexican regional soccer teams; and Mexican or Mexican-American singers, from Maná to Selena.

I spoke openly to the students about my academic commitment to this study, as well as my deep passion for the study itself and for what happens to students like them. However, I did not expect them to necessarily believe me or open up to me without my words being backed up by a further, authentic connection. This came over time, as I slowly "proved" myself to them, not only in the classroom, but on a larger stage, when I participated in a citywide march for immigrant rights, discussed in chapter 5. I already knew some students in room 134 when I returned for my second year of field work. Some were younger siblings of students from the first class, others were good friends of previous students, and had frequently shown up in room 134 to check in with that friend(s). Others I knew from the soccer connection, and there was at least one student who was repeating the class. As noted, I also knew Ms. Lawrence, a white teacher in her mid-40s with more than 20 years teaching experience, the majority at Prairie Heights. She had a good reputation among students in general, and was openly committed to seeing each and every student succeed. This meant many extra hours for her in her classroom before school, at lunch and after school for quick check-ins with students, impromptu tutoring, etc. The students who generally sought her out tended to be the more "plugged-in" students (mostly White) who knew that they had to bring their grades up (or, in more than one case, had been given an ultimatum by their parents). She routinely encouraged the students in room 134 to come to her for help, though not always with success.

Over the course of two school years, Ms. Lawrence's classroom, room 134 at Prairie Heights High School, was the focal point of my afternoons. I was in the classroom for one class three to four days a week during those two years. My general routine was to arrive in room 134 just as the previous class (a traditional Spanish class) was leaving. This gave me time to chat with students more informally and get a sense of what each student might be feeling as they entered room 134. I spent time chatting with students and Ms. Lawrence until the bell rang, and then spent most of my time observing the class and taking brief notes. My physical location in the class varied. I often sat at the back or side of the room. Students seated near me usually felt free to turn around and speak to me if they were doing work at their seats and needed some sort of assistance; in fact, Ms. Lawrence encouraged them to use me as a resource. Other times I was circulating among the small groups Ms. Lawrence had designated, and helping out with a group or given assignment. Ms. Lawrence also routinely asked me to weigh in on particular vocabulary word. Often, as a literary piece or a news report was read for class in Spanish, she would ask students whether or not they knew a different word more commonly used in Mexico, or in their country of origin, that meant the same thing, and she invariably asked me what was most commonly used in Nicaragua. By honoring the students as experts, she granted them status that I discovered was generally not accorded them in their school lives. Drawing me into the conversations created more connections between the students and me, and helped me establish a presence in the classroom. Ms. Lawrence also asked me to offer several lectures to the class on topics including Nicaraguan history, immigration in the United States and Mexican political history.

There seemed to be a fairly high number of new students joining the class, even a good month or two into the semester, due at least in part of the mobility of Latino students in the areas in and around Lakeview. They did not always notice me, although some did. One young man, Fernando, started Ms. Lawrence's class on a day I was not there. The next day, I arrived during passing time, and started settling in. Students entering the class greeted me, several commenting on a few plays during a pick-up soccer game at lunchtime. Fernando came in just as the bell rang, saw me and stopped dead in his tracks. "Quien es ella?, he asked in a dramatic stage whisper. "Y que hace aquí?" In an equally dramatic whisper, though at a somewhat higher volume, Javier hissed, "Ella es la mamá de Jorge." ["Who is she?" "And what is she doing here?" "She's Jorge's mom".] Fernando spun around, walked over to me, stuck out his hand and half-bowed. My role was both accepted and, on some level, parodied. When things got a little too loud in room 134, and things seemed on the brink of 'getting out of hand,' a common reaction was for one of the boys to yell out, relishing their role, however brief, as keeper of order, "*Oye*!!! QUIET. She is studying us, remember?!" A few of the boys were usually quick to point out something that they thought merited recognition. "Write that down, Miss!" was a common interjection from Ricardo or David when they thought someone had said something worth noting.

My observations were invariably intertwined with my knowledge of other schools in Lakeview. At the same time I was carrying out observations and interviews in room 134, I was spending time at Hillside, an elementary school that had one of the largest Latino populations in the district and one of the smallest populations of White students. So I was quite immersed in Lakeview school culture, which deepened and further informed my understanding of the culture and goings-on at Prairie Heights. At Prairie Heights, aside from my ongoing presence in the Spanish for Spanish speakers class, I attended many school-related functions, including parent meetings and school events including sports and fine-arts related, both during and after school hours. I also attended a number of soccer games of the local Latino youth league to see some of the boys from 134 play. And, though of course this was unplanned, Ms. Lawrence and I ended up attending the funeral of a young man who had been very close to several of the boys in room 134, and had been a student of Ms. Lawrence's a year or so earlier. I had seen him play soccer several times, and knew him to be someone that many of the students in room 134 greatly admired (and many attended the funeral). While he should have been a senior, he had dropped out of Prairie Heights, entering a GED program shortly before his death. During my second year at Prairie Heights, two students from my first year in room 134 asked me for assistance with their college and community college applications and I did help them edit and structure their college essays. During my time in 134, I also regularly read several Lakeview blogs dealing with education, including one that regularly included comments from Prairie Heights parents. My time in room 134 was also framed by the political situation in the country and in Lakeview as it affected immigrants and, in particular, immigrant students.

Each year, I initially spent time in Ms. Lawrence's room, simply observing. I explained my project to the students and told them that I hoped to interview a number of students at some point. After some time in the classroom, I approached particular students to see if they would be interested in being interviewed and if their parents would give permission. Ms. Lawrence gave me a fair amount of feedback, indicating students she thought it would be useful to interview. I wanted to include three groups of students; students who were seen as successful students either by teachers or because of their academic records, those students who had already been characterized as 'failing', and as students who were in the middle and with the potential to go either way. I also wanted to have a mix of male and female students. After the first month of both years in room 134, I began to interview students as well. The questions were the same, and ranged from questions about culture and community to how each student saw Prairie Heights and how he or she understood him/herself as a student. Not surprisingly, the interviews deepened my understanding of the students in ways I could not have predicted. One issue that came up time and again was that of legal status; the students did not talk about it at length, but most mentioned it or referred to it. It was also clear in the classroom conversations that the issue of documentation was one that weighed heavily on the students, and greatly informed what they imagined about themselves and their future.

Chapter 3
Remapping Race at Prairie Heights

Forjando una identidad entre dos mundos / **Creating an identity in the space between two worlds**

In this chapter, I argue that the traditional faultlines of race in the Lakeview schools are being redrawn. While Latino students continue to be understood as a sort of 'underclass', raced notions of whiteness privilege these students vis-à-vis their African American peers. Race continues to be a key sorting mechanism, but has morphed from a black-white binary to a more complex, yet still fairly impermeable, system.

A common assertion in the literature regarding racial politics and schooling is that students of color in the US are largely warehoused in schools that are worse – oftentimes, far worse -- than those of their white counterparts. Both advocacy groups, including the NAACP, as well as scholars (Frankenberg, Lee and Orfield, 2003; Kozol, 2005) have advanced this position. Even as the current political discourse claims the advent of a post-racial America, it is true that today we see quite clearly the signs of racial retrenchment as evidenced by increasingly segregated schools, as well as troubling signs in other institutions.[48] At the same time, there is a regrouping or a *remapping* as I term it, as the racial panorama of the US changes. Thus the concern of many scholars, along with those committed to the success of

---

[48] Along with increasingly segregated schools, the health care system, as well as the country's legal systems, and its jails and prisons, show deepening stratification along racial lines.

49

students of color, makes a great deal of sense. Prairie Heights is one of four public high schools in Lakeview, and each of those schools is relatively similar in terms of racial/ethnic demographics. One, albeit somewhat slight, difference is that Prairie Heights has the highest percentage of White students (54%, while the other three schools range from 43- 53%), as well as the lowest percentage of African American students (13%, while the other schools range from 18-24%). The percentage of Latino students in Lakeview's high schools ranges from 12-17%, with Prairie Heights' Latino population at 15%. What does stand out from the demographic statistics is a clear socioeconomic gap among the schools. Looking at the students who come from families that are considered low income, it is quite striking that 'only' 34% of Prairie Heights' population, and 37% of the nearest high school, are from low income families, while the two high schools on the other side of town have low income student populations at, respectively, 57% and 54%. Those schools draw from what was historically the more working class side of town, and the economic divide is still noticeable.[49]

In any case, it is not easy, and neither would it be accurate, to describe any one of the schools in Lakeview as "the" good school. There are National Merit Scholars and other highly ranked students coming out of each of the schools, and they all have programs that routinely win state and/or national recognition for academic excellence and innovation. It is true that Prairie Heights offers a wider range of classes, i.e., foreign language options and more electives, than the other high schools, yet that range of options has come under attack as district administrators push for more uniformity among the high schools. That has been criticized as a return to the more explicit tracking of several decades ago, even sparking some well-organized student sit-ins at one point. This brings us to a particularity of the situation in Lakeview. Each of the schools has students of wealth and privilege alongside poorer and less entitled students. Additionally, each school has a fairly broad range of ethnic/racial diversity. Yet, what we see in school after school, and not exclusively in Prairie Heights, although this phenomenon is quite palpable there, is the sensation of 'two schools

---

[49]This clearly merits further study, as the particular ways in which class and race have intersected in Lakeview continue to have a significant impact on the schools.

within a school.' Students are effectively tracked fairly early on in their academic careers; with some key decisions (particularly in terms of math classes) made in middle school, while other tracking happens only once a student is in high school. And while neither race nor social class play an explicit, or acknowledged, role in this sorting process, it is clear to me from my interaction with the students in room 134 that race does in fact play a decisive role, however disguised. Over the course of the two years I spent at Prairie Heights, race and issues of racialized space and realities in school were a constant, concrete reality, both for me to deal with and understand as a researcher, and of course more palpably and psychically weighty for my students. Although sometimes in a subterranean fashion, race and racial politics clearly informed each student's experience at school.

For years Prairie Heights was considered the more academic school in Lakeview as compared to its main 'rival', Washington High School, across town. Socioeconomic class was the major faultline between the two schools, with Washington understood as the 'lower class' school against the more middle class veneer of Prairie Heights. As the city changed and expanded and the more traditional factory-based jobs left town as companies pulled up stakes and relocated, the divisions between these two sides of Lakeview blurred to a certain degree. Yet, the economic divide persists and today Prairie Heights and another high school several miles down the road consistently have higher graduation rates for their White students, while graduation rates for students of color are fairly uniform and far below their white peers across the board.

So, while in many districts the fear is that students of color are left to their own devices in the 'bad' schools, and the white and/or more economically privileged students are offered educational opportunities, it is a bit more complex in Lakeview, where the sharp dichotomy exists within a single school building. As one example, consider the case of a white student, Justin, who attended and graduated from Prairie Heights and was well known in the school, came from an upper middle-class neighborhood not far from the school. He was able to spend a fair amount of money, some from his parents, some from a part-time job, on expensive soccer equipment and gear, short vacations with his friends, clothes, etc. He was placed in the college-bound track from the time he entered Prairie Heights. By the end of his senior year, he had taken calculus, statistics, advanced physics and successfully completed the AP test in Spanish. He ended up attending the University of Michigan where he has excelled. James, another student from that class, is an African American male. He went to the same middle school as Justin, and was already behind grade level in mathematics by the time he got to Prairie Heights. He had taken only algebra and geometry by the end of his senior year, and though he had taken the 'regular' track physics, his chemistry class gave him problems as he attempted to fill out college applications. The chemistry class he took as a sophomore counted for credits towards his graduation, but neither the state universities nor the local community colleges would accept it. While the community college was willing to admit him, he found that he would have to make up several classes (at the very least, a college semester's worth) as his high school schedule simply had not been rigorous enough. This two-tiered system in Lakeview plays out such that the so-called 'good' or 'motivated' kids often do extremely well and compete easily against their private school counterparts when they go off to selective colleges. It is not only the White kids who do well, and many White kids are also poorly served by this system. Nonetheless, it is quite dramatic to note how far too many kids of color are left behind as race continues to be a prominent sorting mechanism at Prairie Heights.

Prairie Heights is more than 75 years old, and showing the signs of wear and tear. Entering the school during class change can be slightly overwhelming, as the halls are packed with students, alternately rushing to class and taking time to chat up friends. As with any venue housing over 2,000 young people, there is a great sense of energy at Prairie Heights. Kids are talking, yelling, chatting on their phones, greeting friends, couples walking down the hall are sometimes so entwined that a teacher (generally with good humor) urges them to disengage. School security personnel are present though very few are in the vicinity of room 134 on a typical day; they patrol the hall, are often near the school's main entrance or close to the special education classrooms, and frequently joke with the students, many of whom they know by name. Teachers are usually in their doorways (which the administration has explicitly requested of them), monitoring the halls and pushing the students to hurry up and get to class. There are students of all colors, and the physical range from very small 9th graders to hulking upperclassmen borders on the comical. Students' wardrobes range from expensive fashions to second-hand clothes to political t-shirts, athletic jerseys and fairly revealing clothing for some of the girls. Almost anything goes in terms of clothing and there is no 'right' outfit. Students don't pay much attention to one more adult in their midst, but are generally friendly and helpful if asked directions or a similarly straightforward question. In general, the students seem to get along fairly well and while the school is quite large and thus has a somewhat impersonal feeling, the overall impression is one of a busy, yet eminently approachable place, as well as one that appears relatively diverse.

However, a more careful inspection inside the individual classrooms once the halls have cleared reveals a fairly segregated picture, particularly for the upper classmen. After their first year or two at Prairie Heights, those students who are college bound quickly end up in classes where they are with other college bound students all day long except for the required PE classes and some electives; while those students who are not are quickly left 'behind', for the most part. While it is certainly true that not all students should or want to go to college, the decisions are not necessarily made by the students themselves, or their families. Instead, we see a fairly institutionalized, and race-specific, practice of 'gatekeeping' on the part of some counselors, teachers and staff.[50]

When discussing immigrant students and issues of school identity/academic achievement, it may be tempting to look exclusively at language, and to understand the students largely in terms of their lack of English, a common 'deficit' trap that many researchers have warned of.[51] School services tend to be organized around language, and frequently characterize the lack of English as a problem rather than recognizing (and celebrating) Spanish-speaking students as bilingual and bicultural. At the same time, those services rarely officially address some of the other, often key elements that are salient to a student's school experience.

---

[50]This will be discussed at more length in a subsequent chapter.

[51] Lisa Delpit (1988) has been instrumental in guiding many of us to avoid this trap. Valdes (1996) and Ballenger (1999) look specifically at the ways in which a deficit lens is applied to bilingual students.

RACIAL GEOGRAPHY AT PRAIRIE HEIGHTS

Race continues to be a key factor not only in the way students are treated at many schools across the US, but also in terms of how their potential is (or, all too often, not) realized. My observations and interviews indicated that Prairie Heights is no exception. The students I interviewed entered a school with a particular racial history, in a city with a cloaked racial discourse, and while they were afforded entrance, they have not been awarded full status. As noted earlier, Prairie Heights is in many ways two schools within one school building. The Prairie Heights attendance area includes some of Lakeview's wealthiest areas, as well as some of the poorest areas in the city. The Prairie Heights students from families with highly educated parents and a great deal of disposable income have a real sense, often borne out by reality, that the school district 'belongs' to them.

Lakeview's fair housing ordinances were not enacted until the mid-1960s and a state of ongoing segregation reigned in the elementary and middle schools until the early 1980s. There was little explicit thought or lip service paid to diversity in the 1960s and 70s, and many of Prairie Heights' African-American students were 'graduated' without the skills or academic foundation necessary to go on to post-secondary education. Star athletes were often well recognized in the school community, but given no support structure when they experienced academic difficulties. Prairie Heights, in fact, was quite notorious in the 1980s for its extremely poor graduation rates among African-American students.

Prairie Heights is a school that was racially 'static' for many years. Perhaps in part due to its location in a particular area of Lakeview, the school has a decidedly White, middle-class culture. The core of the school in terms of power dynamics is a group of parents from the upper middle class area surrounding the school, as well as from several similar neighborhoods at a slight distance. These parents run the parent-teacher organization, do ongoing fundraising for the school, have constant access to the administration and are extremely vocal about the way they want things done at 'their' school.[52] While that is certainly a

---

[52] A principal at one of Lakeview's elementary schools described the parent-teacher organizations as "white, middle-class and female bastions of power".

laudable cause, it is apparent that their voices tend to drown out the others; they are seen as more 'reasonable', more educated, and, quite importantly, as 'better parents'. I attended go-to-school nights, and several grade-level parent meetings during the time I was carrying out my research at Prairie Heights. Very few parents of color attended those events, and while there were probably a number of reasons, the fact that many of them did not feel welcome certainly had an impact. Aside from the announcements in school bulletins, e-mails and automated phone reminders, I was unaware of any specific plan to reach out to the parents of color, although several teachers remarked to me that they were concerned that it was always the 'same' people in attendance at many school-related functions, wondering what the school could do to turn that around.

One could argue that by the time students get to Prairie Heights; the die, for all practical purposes, is cast. Many students of color, particularly male students, are routinely constructed as 'troublemakers' or boys with "bad attitudes" as young children. While the Lakeview district has made several attempts over the past 20 years or so to more equitably serve its African-American students, it remains a serious, latent issue. The fact that racial inequalities have not been successfully dealt with, much less resolved, in either the school district or the surrounding community, has had a great impact on the way Latino students are understood. Ramirez (2010) discusses the category of *designated losers,* noting that students of color are expected to fail and, indeed, must fail if the system is to continue relatively unchallenged or unchanged. Her conceptualization of the long-term consequences of brutally low expectations is both relevant and useful in the context of Prairie Heights. The Latino students provide a foil, as it were, and allow the white teachers and thus, the White, racialized system, to feel that they have done right by one group of students they implicitly understand as 'other.' However, those Latino students are largely *not* allowed access to real power as in access to post-secondary options, though they are constructed as 'better', or 'easier' minority students than the African American students who remain firmly on the bottom. What might, in the best of worlds, have been a shake-up has actually solidified racial separation at Prairie Heights.

Along with this, historically the ELL students in the district have been concentrated at Prairie Heights and its feeder schools, as most ELL students in the district were from families affiliated with the university; 'culture' was afforded a very different status in that context. The ELL students in the district were from well educated families, were clearly in the numerical minority and as one former ELL student (who later returned to Lakeview as an adult) said, "We were all going to leave, one day or another." Today's ELL students are mostly immigrants and are here for the foreseeable future. While they have much investment in the wisdom and necessity of getting a good education, many of them come from families where the parents may not have finished grade school, much less high school. The parents work long hours and their immediate concern is providing for their families.

As discussed earlier, Lakeview's schools have undergone tremendous demographic change in the last 20-25 years. A sizable number of Hmong students are enrolled in schools throughout the district, and Lakeview's African-American population has increased[53] as well. It was not until the late 1990s that Latino students began to be a statistically important population within the district, and by midway through the first decade of this century, Latino students made up over 10% of the district's total population, a figure which is nearing 20% at this writing. Prairie Heights has experienced fairly rapid changes in its racial/ethnic demographics over the last years, and some of its feeder schools have experienced particularly dramatic changes, which have led to a high degree of 'white flight' either out of specific schools or away from the district itself.

However, although the school district is quite diverse demographically, the mindset of the district remains little changed over

---

[53]This is a point of ongoing controversy within Lakeview. Many of Lakeview's white citizens blame increasing racial tensions and a widening achievement gap on new groups of African-American students who have arrived with their families from larger, urban areas. This ends up being a convenient way to sidestep the issue of how to effectively deal with the problems; students are often written off as 'unteachable' or 'intransigent.' This perspective also assumes that there was an ideal moment in Lakeview's history in which racial tensions and conflict simply did not exist.

the last decades. The normative culture remains a white, middle-class[54] culture, and the diversity that is so apparent on paper is not necessarily enacted in the school setting. Indeed, racial faultlines continue to be fundamental dividers. This is apparent, for instance, when one considers the makeup of the Advanced Placement or honors, classes. Most of the students in those classes are white and from middle or upper-class families. Many are college-bound and will find themselves in quite segregated math classes from 9th grade on, with the segregation gradually increasing so that by the time college-bound students are juniors, there are often almost no students of color in the more academically difficult classes. This is extremely isolating for those few students of color who do make it into the college-bound classes.[55]

A clear separation between Black and White students has existed for quite a long time at Prairie Heights; my sense is that the gap in many ways continues to widen despite the many often well-intentioned, if not particularly effective, programs aimed at confronting issues of inequality. While a number of Black students do make it through school and do quite well during their time at Prairie Heights, those who do not occupy a sort of no-man's zone within the school.

The way in which the school quickly sorts students was underscored when I attended an informational meeting for parents during the second year of my research at Prairie Heights. One of the assistant principals offered a rundown on the incoming sophomore class, noting, by percentages, how many students had 4.0 GPAs, 3.5 GPAs and on down the line. He then mentioned a sizeable group of well over 50 students "who have already dug themselves into a hole so deep they will have a hard time getting out." While that group was not exclusively students of color, they were the majority. There is much

---

[54] I have heard class and race both conflated and used interchangeably or as codes by both parents and teachers in the district, often in ways that attribute any and all issues raised around race to socio-economic status; this claim seems to me to be visibly unfounded.

[55] Adela talked about this a number of times. She wanted to stay in Ms. Lawrence's Spanish class instead of enrolling in the AP Spanish class because she wanted "one place where I can just feel like me." She ended up taking the AP class, and did very well, but it did take an emotional toll on her.

evidence from the Lakeview district to indicate that students of color who fail, or otherwise fall through the cracks, not only suffer academic consequences but are far more likely to be sucked into the juvenile justice system than their white counterparts.

This is the situation encountered by Latino students entering Prairie Heights. These students and their peers at other schools throughout the district are part of a demographic change that has introduced another variable into the traditional black-white equation that has held for so many years. Many of the students have been in the district long enough that their experience with race at Prairie Heights is not the first time they have dealt with race relations at a US school. However, race tends to play out differently at the high school level[56] and that, along with the sheer size of the school, and the students' maturity, makes it a rather more potent factor in their daily school lives.

While most of the students I spoke with come from a country with its own and complicated racial history, one marked difference between that and their high school experience is that they will always be the *other* at Prairie Heights. Their daily class period in room 134 created a space of acceptance and comfort, but that did not extend beyond the borders of the room. At first glance, one might characterize the 134 students as, in essence, invisible, while in fact it is the opposite. As they are so clearly 'othered' by the school's highly racialized system, they are hyper-visible. Yet their constant presence as "other" secures them neither status nor power.

As students entered room 134 every day, there was a level of comfort and ease, as if they were entering a sanctuary of sorts. Emilio was outgoing, funny and engaged in class, yet I would sometimes see him in the hall or at larger school-related events; in those situations, he was quiet and withdrawn. I asked him about it. "Es que con Miss Lawrence, me siento bien, aquí estamos entre amigos." ["With Miss (*sic*) Lawrence, I feel fine; we're among friends here".] As room 134 students entered the class each day, a Spanish class for non-native speakers, overwhelmingly White students, was filing out. While there

---

[56]This is not to say that race and racial politics are not constants at the elementary and middle school levels, but rather that at those levels, particularly elementary school, students may not be directly aware of the racial politics that shape and constrict their interactions at school.

was no hostility between the two groups of students, there was also little conversation or interaction.

Most of the students I spoke with did not think that Prairie Heights had completely opened its doors to them. Though they are not talking about race at every moment, it is a constant reference when they describe other students, staff and teachers. The word most commonly used to refer to white teachers and students is *"güero"* with *"blanco"* a close second.[57] Though many of the students had positive things to say about the school, it was clear that they also felt fairly distant from the locus of power and activity at the school. They were often unaware of, or were uninterested in, events such as plays and musical performances, and sporting events that were drawing in scores of other students. While there are many White students who do not participate in these sorts of traditional school activities, the students in room 134 understood their own lack of involvement at that level as at least partially linked to race. Student after student described many of the school's extracurricular events as *white*. When I asked Victor if he ever went to sporting events, school plays or concerts, he seemed a little surprised. "No, I'm just not that interested."[58] The one student who regularly went to school events was Natalia, who was dating a White student throughout her junior and senior years. Unlike their peers who thrived on school, receiving recognition and being able to recharge their batteries on a daily basis, so to speak, they lived a life parallel to the life at school, and much of what they did, from social events to church attendance to soccer games in the local Latino league, was neither recognized nor honored by the school.[59] This is despite the

---

[57] *Güero* is Mexican slang for anyone with white skin or blond hair. While it is not necessarily derogatory, some of the students clearly used it to be so. *Blanco* simply means white.

[58] "No, es que no me interesan tanto." All translations into English are mine. If no Spanish translation is provided, it is because the student was speaking in English. "

[59] I do not mean to suggest that students must have or should seek an official or implied school stamp of approval for their activities outside of school; I merely suggest that all students should benefit from the kind of recognition and support currently afforded only to some.

fact that a number of individual teachers have made strong and lasting connections to these students, and there are some whom the students cited as the sole reason they remained in school. Sonia, for example, talked about her first year at Prairie Heights. "I was in that study class, you know, with Ms. P," she said, referring to a class intended to help ease students' transition to school, taught by a teacher who has a reputation for going out of her way to make contact with kids. "But I really wasn't studying. Actually, I almost never came to class. So Ms. P. says to me one day, "Just come. Don't worry about the work or anything. Just come. Just show up." And I did. And she didn't make me feel stupid or anything. She really *wanted* me there." In Sonia's other classes, however, the end results were disheartening, as she felt that the teachers didn't like her or didn't make any attempt to connect with her. Even though it ended up hurting her more than anything, her response was to frequently skip class. She ended up with quite poor grades that year, and those grades were still weighing her down by the time I met her two years later.

At the same time, the unspoken discourse of lowered expectations and inaccurate attitudes about Latino students and their lives takes an enormous toll on students. Race and its consequences are an ever present reality, one from which students are simply unable to retreat. In a few conversations with White students who were peers of Ms. Lawrence's Spanish-speaking students, a number of them often unwittingly pointed to some of the key problems facing their Latino counterparts. One very popular student and athlete noted that, "Nobody really pays attention to them," an opinion seconded by a number of his friends. Another student described them as "a different sect," adding that she tried to speak Spanish with them with some success. They all quickly added that this wasn't fair, or a good situation, but "that's just how it is." One student lamented that the Latino students were 'often excluded,' while another student said that it was "great" and "cool" to have other students from '"different" places at Prairie Heights and said, "Everyone has a different story" that makes Prairie Heights "better" and "more diverse." Another student felt that the Latino students "...just don't fit in," and wondered why they "always speak Spanish to each other."

When asked if they knew any Spanish-speaking students, they all mentioned students they had met through Ms. Lawrence's TA program[60] or one of the biracial, Anglo-Latino students at the school, a few of whom were well known as athletes or theater people. The white students' estimates of how many Latino students attended Prairie Heights ranged from 100 to 1000 (that would have been half the school); it was actually just over 200 at the time. When asked why so many Latino students had come to Prairie Heights in recent years, few of the white students had any idea; one said, "I guess their parents need jobs, but why would they come *here*?"

Prairie Heights is part of a school district that routinely graduates just over half of its students of color. There are stark and visible racial faultlines at the school in terms of special education students, disciplinary issues, and students in the advanced or honors classes. Student 'talk' indicated to me the very real and often disturbing ways in which the immigrant students have absorbed and to some degree accepted the great degree of racial separation that prevails in the school[61]. The students in room 134 made frequent and disparaging remarks about their African-American peers, criticized them for not working hard enough, for causing trouble, and the like; in short, they repeated the charges leveled against many African American youth in the local and national media, and embedded as well in the attitudes of many in the school system. They largely intuit that the racial stratification at school is one of the key, if not the only, axes of power and it was clearly understood that White, wealthier kids, who were sometimes described to me in terms of geography and sometimes in terms of what they 'did' as a particular sport or extracurricular activity, were the ones holding the lion's share of power at the school. Oscar talked about the different ways that status and power were expressed at

---

[60] For several years, Ms. Lawrence offered native Spanish speakers the chance to volunteer for non-GPA credit in her classroom and help her with the Spanish-language students. The program was a huge success and did much to begin to build relationships between the native Spanish speakers and a number of the other students at Prairie Heights. The program was cancelled when an administrator imposed a minimum GPA for any potential volunteer; none of the volunteers met the criteria and thus their disengagement from school and the school community deepened.

[61] This issue is very ably described by Olsen (1997) and others.

Prairie Heights. "The people who do the most here are the ones who put a lot of time into school and are successful, but the ones with the most power are the ones who are most popular, although that's not the way it should be ... they're all higher class, most of them are White."[62]

It is interesting that Oscar, and other students in room 134, understood the underlying class realities, but *saw* race. Maria saw similar divisions, noting, "Los populares son blancos," ["the popular kids are white"] although she was more nuanced in her assessment of the many differences among white students, something that no other student in room 134 mentioned. "There are a lot of groups that have to do with personal interests, they have something in common, there is a group known as the geeks, there are punks and Goths, they express their own ideas."[63] It was clear to me from a number of school events such as sports rallies and fine arts that the White culture of the school had a complicated and often contradictory stance towards Prairie Heights' African-American students. African-American students were among the most popular students in the school; all of them were either good football or basketball athletes or well-known as members of the school's drama programs, and elicited the loudest applause and cheers, both at fine arts events and pep rallies for the school teams. Many of these students were doing well in school, though few of them were considered top scholars. However, the majority of the African-American students at Prairie Heights were dismissed by the school culture. They were not very engaged in school classes or extracurricular activities and there was an unstated perception that they themselves were the cause of their lack of status and success.

Not surprisingly, the Latino students in room 134 picked up on this dynamic. Though they all pointed to *"los americanos"* or *"los blancos"* as the ones having real power at the school, they seemed to have scant interaction with any of the White students. When I asked

---

[62]"Las personas que hacen más aquí son las que se meten mucho tiempo en el colegio y son exitosos, pero los con más poder son las que son más populares, aunque no es correcto ... todos son de más alto nivel económico, la mayoría son blancos."

[63] "Hay muchos grupos que tienen que ver con los intereses personales, tienen algo en común, hay como un grupo que los llaman *geeks*, hay *punks* y *Goths*, se expresan sus propios ideas."

them to describe the breakdown of power and status among students in the school, a number of them described tensions between African-American and Mexican students.[64] Those tensions were quite pronounced the first year of my research at Prairie Heights, with several fights involving several dozen students taking place within a few months' span, and all the fights breaking down along racial lines. Many of the students I interviewed talked about their African-American peers as students they had to confront, or somehow 'beat out', to ensure their own success. Only David talked about having close African-American friends. He had transferred from a middle school in a town outside of Lakeview to a middle school with a large African-American population and he talked about his middle school principal as a "cool dude" who tried to bring all the kids together. David was still close to several of his African-American friends from middle school and they in turn opened doors for him to a wider group of friends at Prairie Heights.

As our conversations continued, it became clear that the 134 students thought that as a group, the African American students were on the bottom of the social and academic hierarchy. If they were able to hopscotch over them, so to speak, they gained a foothold, however tenuous, at Prairie Heights. Oscar discussed his African American peers in a conversation one day, "Well, it's true that there are gangs here, it's pretty easy to get caught up in bad things, and to a certain degree they respect you then, they leave you alone ... there's a big distance between the blacks, the whites and the Mexicans ... to be honest, the reason that there's so much tension between the Blacks and the Mexicans is because we're equal."[65] He uses the word *morenos*, which literally means brown, to refer to the African-American students and

---

[64]The terms "Mexican" and "Latino" were both often used by the Mexican students to refer to themselves. "Latino" was claimed by only some of the Mexican students, and all of the Central and Latin American students.

[65] "Bueno, es cierto que hay pandillas aquí, es muy fácil de involucrarse con cosas malas, y en cierto sentido te respetan, y te dejan en paz ... hay mucha separación entre los morenos, los gueros y los mexicanos ... francamente la razón por lo que hay tensión entre los morenos y los mexicanos es que los dos somos iguales."

calls the White students *gueros*. And while some students did use the term Latino, he uses Mexican. He described the *morenos* as a threat to him at school, noting that some of them didn't want him and the other *Mexicanos* to do well or succeed.

When I asked about the White students and where *they* fit, the Latino students seemed to think that the White students were virtually unassailable in terms of their status and power at the school. Oscar thought that he and other Latino students had a harder time getting ahead than their White peers did. "I don't think that we have the same opportunities, Oscar stated, adding that "a lot of Latinos come here and look, they put them in these really easy classes that don't lead to anything."[66] The students realized that the power with which they dealt was not solely attributable to race, but rather the importance of social class and wealth. At Prairie Heights, there was a tendency for many teachers to conflate poverty and race, and for some of the students in room 134, that was an easy trap into which to fall, and one probably made easier because a number of the high profile students at Prairie Heights were both White and fairly well off.

Interestingly, the many White students who also fell through the cracks did not really factor into the students' discussion of the power hierarchies at school; when I pointed out that many White students were not necessarily well-served by the school, the most common reaction was one of disbelief. Luis summed up the internal division at Prairie Heights by verbally sketching a break-down of the student population for me: "First, the Mexicans, the Chicanos, then the Blacks, the ones who play basketball, there are more Blacks than Mexicans, then the Asians. The Hmong, the Chinese, I don't see any differences, but they say there are differences; I guess they also speak different languages and then the Americans – the preppies, they do what they want, because of their color and their money."[67] He noted that most

---

[66] Yo pienso que no tenemos las mismas oportunidades; muchos Latinos vienen acá y ven que les dan puros clases faciles, que no lleva a nada."

[67] "Primero, los mexicanos, los chicanos, luego los morenos, los que juegan basketball, más morenos que mexicanos, después los asiáticos (los hmong, los chinos, yo no noto diferencias, pero dicen que hay diferencias, me imagino que hablan lenguajes diferentes tambien) y

teachers treat "los morenos y los mexicanos" very differently, adding that, "piensan que vamos a ser algo mal, siempre, sospechan a nosotros, y a los morenos." [...they always think we're going to do something bad, they suspect us, and the Black students...] Oscar's comments touched more on potential conflicts between Latino and African-American students. "There's a lot of separation among Blacks, Whites and Mexicans, there's a lot of tension between the Blacks and Mexicans at times, more than with other groups; honestly, the reason there's tension between the Blacks and the Mexicans is that they are two equal groups; they both think that their culture is better and neither of them are going to back down."[68]

Speaking in broader societal terms, but with insight relevant to the schools in Lakeview, Gans points to what he calls an "apparently increasing white tolerance for racial differences, except with respect to blacks." (Gans, 2009, p. 122) At two local elementary schools which I had occasion to visit numerous times during same time period that I was carrying out my research, I saw young African American boys essentially hounded into failure. Even those boys who were treated fairly and had positive elementary school experiences could logically expect to find more problems at the middle and high school level, as the stakes increase. Their families often had to fight for them in ways not expected, or demanded, of White parents.[69] After many conversations with teachers at one elementary school that feeds into Prairie Heights, it was disconcerting to realize that there is an increasing but not yet widespread sense that the Latino kids are the

---

después los americanos – los preppy, hacen lo que quieren por su color y su dinero ..."

[68] "Hay mucha separación de morenos, gueros y mexicanos, hay mucha tensión entre los morenos y los mexicanos a veces, más que otro grupo ... francamente la razón por lo que hay tensión entre los morenos y los mexicanos es que los dos son muy iguales, los dos piensan que su cultura es lo mejor; y ni los mexicanos ni los morenas se van a dejar."

[69] A White teacher who felt powerless to change the school culture beyond her classroom made this statement to me.

'good' minority.[70] The white students remain unassailable, but perhaps more importantly the African American students are even more firmly located on the very bottom rung of the school ladder. At this feeder school a young African American child who had been homeless for at least 6 months enrolled at the school; although I had no need to hear an assessment, he was described as violent, troubled and manipulative. He reacted angrily to teachers who attempted to make him behave, but yet was childlike and relaxed with one of the educational aides, a young woman who radiated a sense of both strength and calm. It was a chilling illustration of how expectations work, and how quickly young children are channeled into very rigid roles, which they will all too likely learn to perform with skill. I saw similar issues in several elementary schools in the Lakeview school district, which had experienced a rapid growth in the population of Latino students in recent years. Latino students were routinely, and almost invariably, described to me as 'nicer,' 'better behaved,' and having more parental support and 'stronger' families than their African-American peers. It seemed more comfortable for teachers to approach and work with their Latino students. Perhaps this might be because they were able to position themselves in the role of "helping" the Latino students and their families, whom they construed, with good intentions, as in need of "help" and "charity." At the same time, it was equally clear to me that the Latino students were still seen as occupying space "under" or "less important" than the White students, and here I should clarify that I mean a certain *kind* of White student; the combination of race, social class and educational status seemed to propel a certain type of parent and thus the students into positions of real power within the school. In essence, the hierarchy remained unchanged at the top.

In my ongoing observations of the Spanish for Spanish speakers students at Prairie Heights, I saw the ways in which race and racial politics played an ongoing role in the students' daily lives. Most days before class began, as students filed in, talking and joking with each

---

[70] As I am using the phrase, the 'good minority' should in no way be confused with the research on 'model minority.' Additionally, this is not even a conscious or deliberate shift on the part of many teachers, but rather it seems to be the 'logical' or 'natural' way for them to understand this new group of students.

other (this was, for many of the students, a brief respite from their day – the only time during the school day when they could be exclusively with other Spanish speakers and just as importantly, with kids "like" themselves), the comments and jokes often centered around issues of race. One student who was frequently in trouble with his other teachers routinely arrived at class complaining about those teachers. "A mi no me quieren porque soy mexicano", Ricardo would claim on more than one occasion, arguing that one of his teachers didn't like him "because he was Mexican." Though other students would sometimes tease him, wondering if maybe the fact that he often didn't do his homework had something to do with the problem, his sense was that being Mexican set him apart, and resonated strongly with the other students in a distinctly negative way.

Many of the other students had stories to tell, including one told to me several times, once by the affected student himself and other times by classmates offended on his behalf. Javier related how he was rushing upstairs to class one day as he was worried about being late; "See, miss?" he proclaimed. "That's how much I like this class".[71] The stairwells are packed during class change time as the school is sizeable, and it is difficult for students to get from one class to the next on time, even if they lag even a minute extra to talk to friends in the hall or with a teacher after class. A student rushing through the halls or up or down a staircase is not something that would be thought to cause comment or much notice. However, one of the school's security guards bodily blocked Javier that day. "None of the guards are Latino", he told me, and also underscored the fact that he liked the one African American bodyguard more than the white guards, in part because that guard "tries to speak Spanish."

He was stopped and a strong hand pulled him up a stair, and kept a tight grip on his shoulder. Without saying much to him (it was quickly clear that the bodyguard assumed he did not speak English), the bodyguard used his walkie-talkie to communicate with another guard in the school. "I'm pretty sure it's him," he said. "Well, it's *one* of those Mexican kids," and went on to describe a robbery that had taken place

---

[71] Many of the students associated me with the class and seemed to want to prove to me that they were indeed engaged with, and committed to, the class.

in the morning and how now he "had" the perpetrator. Javier let him rattle on a bit, then began to speak and defend himself, in perfectly comprehensible English. According to Javier, the guard was shocked and let him go, but the lesson was not lost on Javier or his friends; for at least some of the school staff, including those who have extra power over students' lives, the Mexican students are seen as an essentially nameless mass, remarkable only in that they are 'troublemakers' and somehow outside the bounds of the legitimate student body.

If we understand one fundamental contribution of Critical Race Theory to be the way in which it posits the intersection of race and property as providing a crucial analytical tool to understanding both societal and school-based inequality, it is also useful to conceive of the particular position of immigrant students in schools as one informed equally and dramatically by both race and property. The students I spoke with are often painfully cognizant of their position in school. They realize that the power and status conferred on white students is probably unattainable, but understand as well that more than "just" race is at play. If we think of property as it played out in the foundation of this country, the setting down of roots, which were then legally denied to many others because of their race, ethnicity or lack of economic wherewithal, we can look at the situation of many immigrants today as mirroring that. While immigrants have access to property *per se*, they are effectively barred from the full status historically granted to property owners. As described in another chapter, the legal status of immigrants in this country and in schools all across the nation becomes a bludgeon wielded against them to ensure that they do not climb the mythical ladder said to be accessible to all and so central to the deep mythologies about success and justice in the US.

Student talk before class started and in the down moments during class indicated to me that there were serious tensions among the Latino students. I usually arrived at room 134 while the earlier class was still in session, precisely to be able to hear the students' ideas of the 'news of the day'. The students absorbed the racial framework even as they were becoming part of it, absorbing, among other things, a fairly stereotypical view of racial/ethnic groups and roles, although they often had friendships that exploded those stereotypes; the reality of race and racial politics played a large role in the way they treated and understood each other. Issues of skin color, 'acting white' and where each student fit into the larger racial hierarchy were issues that informed and affected student perception and experience at school.

Oscar was a student who came up against the often complex racial politics of the Mexican community within schools. A fairly big guy, he was not easily pushed around. He had a strong sense of his Mexican identity, as well as a strong and sometimes crushing sense of his responsibility to his family, particularly his younger siblings. He was the oldest of four children, and clearly understood himself as his family's link to success and stability in the US.[72] During my formal interview with Oscar, he often spoke in a voice that was nearly inaudible. He clearly had intense feelings about much of what he was saying, as he began to describe to me the tremendous pressure he had faced as a freshman at Prairie Heights. *"Los mexicanos,"* he told me, clarifying that he was referring to *"los otros,"* or the others, not the kind of Mexican he felt himself to be. He explained in more depth that he thought that a number of Mexican students were gang affiliated, a belief seconded out by some teacher comments[73], and were pressuring him and other students to be "more Mexican"; according to Oscar this meant "not doing shit in school," not speaking English and generally identifying as exclusively Mexican. "There are gangs here ... if you're a freshman, the seniors are gonna pick on you, you have no right to speak up, the older ones want to put you down ... and an easy way to get them to take you seriously is to get involved with bad things, with gangs, with people like that." [74]

---

[72]Both of Oscar's parents worked long hours, and spoke almost no English. I met them at a school event for Latino parents where Oscar received an award. They were clearly proud of his success at school, and mentioned several times that they hoped he would not have to suffer and struggle as they had.

[73]Interestingly, his contention was also supported by another student at Prairie Heights who told me he was 'let off the hook' when the Mexican *pandilleros,* or gang members, realized that he was Central American.

[74] "Hay pandillas aquí...si eres un freshman, los seniors they're gonna pick on you, tu no tienes derecho de hablar, la gente mayor quieren verte abajo ... y una manera muy fácil de que te toman en serio es involucrarse con cosas malas, con pandilleros, con personas así..."

Ironically, Oscar's own Mexican identity, as mentioned above, was very strong and was something that he claimed for himself with a great deal of pride. However, he was willing to deal with extreme pressure from some of his peers as he staked his claim to academic success and moved fairly easily between languages, and to a lesser extent, between cultures. He managed to stave off the pressure his entire high school career.

Victor alluded to the same pressure as Oscar, and explained one reason *he* had largely been able to evade it. "If you're small, you know they're going to pick on you; if you're bigger, they leave you alone."[75] One day in the hallway, however, the pressure nearly got to Oscar. According to Ms. Lawrence, Justin, the previously mentioned White soccer player, ran into her classroom during a class change to tell her that one of "her" students was in trouble. She found Oscar and two other Mexican boys in the middle of the hall, facing off against each other. One was muttering rude, vulgar insults while the other seemed to be preparing for a fight. The two boys were goading Oscar into a fight and, although worried about stepping in physically, Ms. Lawrence desperately tried to calm Oscar down; as she told me later, "He didn't seem to hear a thing." She continued talking, pleading, "Don't mess up your scholarship," and told Justin, "Did you know he is in the running for a full ride?"[76] Justin turned to him, and said, "Wow! Congratulations, dude." That somehow stopped Oscar in his tracks and he said, "thanks", turned and walked away.

When I asked the students to talk explicitly about power, *not* race, the discussion inevitably turned to racial politics. Victor saw the racial structure this way: "At Prairie Heights, the *gavachos* are the highest group; the Whites have more power because they are the majority; one time we were accused of breaking a window, but they never, never accused the White kids who were there, too; it depends on how many Latinos there are, and how many White kids."[77]

---

[75] "Si eres chiquito, sabes que te van a pick on you, si estás más grande, no se meten contigo."

[76] Oscar did end up getting a full scholarship to a small Catholic college in the region.

[77] "en Prairie Heights, los gavachos son el grupo más alto ... los blancos tiene más poder por ser mayoría ...; una vez nos acusaron de

While Victor and Oscar both had the advantage of size and knowing English fairly well, some of the other boys suffered more. Emilio, for instance, was a young man who came to the US as a 14-year-old. He offered two different accounts on different occasions and was not clear about how far he had gone in school while still in Mexico, but it was clear that he was struggling academically. He had a very gentle spirit, but could rise to anger quickly when taunted by the other boys which he said happened frequently. He told me that the other boys were from a specific gang and that none of them were from room 134, a fact I could not verify. They made fun of him because of his short stature, and they also constantly rode him about joining their gang. Emilio's mother was indigenous and barely spoke Spanish[78] and he had left her and several younger siblings back in Mexico with the goal of sending her money on a regular basis, which he did. Victor had commented that any student who had to work was at a disadvantage in school, and his comment spoke poignantly to Emilio's situation. Victor also said, "It is much more difficult for the immigrants, and the minorities; they have to work a lot and their families also have to work a lot; it's like they're different at school, they're like the *rejects, nobody talks to them.*"[79]

While part of the students' isolation came from the fact that they were not afforded full, or even partial, entrance into the mainstream school culture, there was also tension *among* the Latino students. Luis referred to the language conflicts that he saw played out among his peers. "I don't know... the thing is that there are two kinds of

---

romper a una ventana, pero no, pero por qué no acusaron a los blancos que estaban allá tambien, depende en cuántos latinos hay, y cuántos blancos". *Gavacho* is a term used to refer to Whites, and while it can sometimes be used rather derogatorily; it most often is used in a primarily descriptive way.

[78] Escárcega and Varese (2004) discuss the ongoing and significant influence of Mixtec culture among many Mexican immigrant families, noting that it is fairly common to find families where Spanish is the second language, and often one not fully mastered.

[79]"Es mucho más difícil para los inmigrantes, y los minorías, tienen que trabajar mucho y sus familias tambien tienen que trabajar mucho, son como diferentes en el colegio, son como rejects, nadie les hablan ..."

Mexicans, some say hat they are "the" Mexicans, and they say that we are chicanos because we speak a lot of English, even though we were born there, sometimes there are fights ... they are the biggest group, they are the ones who came one or two years ago, or even more recently."[80]   David talked fairly eloquently about what it means to claim a particular identity. "It's not just acting Latino, I'm just saying if you're little, you grow up with white people and stuff, so how are you gonna hang out with Latino people when you're older?? Like I went to elementary, I hung out with my cousins, then in middle school, 'cause I spoke more English, it seems that I hung out with white people in 6th grade, but in 7th grade I started hanging out with Latino people; I started being Latino again. The white people still talked to me and stuff and said hi, but it wasn't the same no more."

Camila came from the Southern Cone, was somewhat isolated from the rest of the class and seen as somehow apart from the others.[81] However, two students from the Andean region did not deal with the same lack of integration into the small classroom community, in part because they looked "more Mexican"; one of the Mexican students mentioned this to me when a staff member came into the class for administrative reasons and mistakenly took those two students for Mexican, but correctly assumed that Camila was not. This could also be understood as looking "less white." It was clear as well that Camila routinely set herself apart from the other students, distancing herself from the Mexican students as much as she could. There are some very white-skinned Mexican students at the school, and some racial

---

[80] "Yo no sé, es que aquí hay dos tipos de mexicanos, unos dicen que ellos son "los" mexicanos, y nos dicen que somos chicanos porque hablamos mucho inglés, aunque nacimos allí, a veces hay pleitos ... ellos son el grupo más grande, son gente que llegaron hace 1-2 años, o incluso menos."

[81] The very few Lakeview and Prairie Heights students from the Southern Cone countries had come to the US on airplanes, with some sort of papers. In Camila's case, she was very white-skinned and spoke a different dialect of Spanish. Fairly or unfairly, the other students saw her as somewhat snobbish. This was compounded by the fact that many of her friends were White.

differences seem to be erased by the fact that all Mexican students sense themselves thrown together in the eyes of the school.

POWER AT PRAIRIE HEIGHTS

In both my observations of the students and my one-on-one interviews with them, the race factor came up repeatedly. While it wasn't necessarily the most salient or only factor affecting their lives in school, it was certainly one of the most important. I asked each of my interviewees to describe or map out for me the hierarchy of power and status at school. Without exception, all of the students described and understood whiteness as connoting power and status within the school. Several even talked exclusively about the white kids as they pointed to powerful groups at school. Maria, for example, mentioned "los geek," and "los punk," as well as some of the groups associated more with theater or particular sports. "The majority in these groups are White, the popular kids are White, the ones who do sports, who are more *outgoing.*"[82] Groups that formed outside the formal school structure and centered around particular interests (i.e., the so-called geeks and punks) were almost exclusively White. Football, and to a lesser extent basketball, transcended race, although the basketball team was also somewhat problematic in that it was barely integrated and had acquired a reputation for being a team with almost no academic standing. Race and athletics has been a longstanding issue at Prairie Heights, although historically this was understood solely as a black-white issue. However, one of the most high status sports at the school today is soccer and that brings with it many particularities about how soccer has played out in the community of Lakeview; its origins go back to university-linked players and several upper middle-class families in Lakeview and the surrounding communities who helped found youth soccer leagues some 40 years ago. Soccer training starts early in Lakeview and most of the kids who make it onto the varsity squads of their high school teams have played club soccer since age 6 or 7. This cuts out many of the Mexican students, who are undoubtedly some of the best players in the city, but are not involved in the traditional club leagues.

---

[82] "La mayoría son blancos de estos grupos …los populares son blancos, los que hagan deportes, son más outgoing."

Additionally, the residency rules that athletes must follow to play sports in the Lakeview schools do not necessarily make sense for the kind of mobility that is common in Latino families in the area; that sort of mobility is virtually unheard of in the more economically stable families who own spacious homes in prime neighborhoods throughout Lakeview. Javier was a phenomenal soccer player, but never hit it off with the coach, who was not willing to cut him any slack in terms of making tryout times which were held in early August when Javier was still working full-time; most of the other boys didn't even have to think about juggling work and sports. "I love to play," he told me one day, "I don't know why here everything is about who you know, your family..."[83] He experienced his beloved game as something beyond his reach in the school setting, and quickly soured on the program in general.

The overwhelming majority of my male interviewees and at least several of the girls played soccer in the city's Latino leagues. While this is extremely positive in terms of community, it is also something that almost nobody at school is even aware of, and so is not easily translated into any kind of status at school. This is a vital point as so much in high school hinges on recognition and how your peers see you. Also, of course, if one is not in a school-sponsored sport, there is no way to demand academic accountability. School athletes have to turn in weekly reports during their seasons to ensure that they are doing well in school attending and also passing all their classes. If they fail to do so, they can be sanctioned and may miss a game or number of games. It has been a largely effective way to keep participating athletes on track during their seasons, but has little impact on those involved in sports outside the school structure.

A phenomenon long seen in the public schools throughout Lakeview has been the inability of the system to deal effectively with students of color—even though many individual White teachers do well with individual students of color. There is much fear and lack of cultural understanding in this arena and this has historically led to teachers expect far too little from students of color. Tremaine, an African-American student at Prairie Heights, described how teachers

---

[83] "A mi me encanta jugar, no sé por qué aquí todo tiene que ver con quien conoce, tu familia..."

routinely praise him for doing a minimal amount of work, and demand very little of him. He was close to graduating when he told me that he had such a poor GPA that he had enrolled in a community college to make up several of the courses that he should have easily passed in high school; his story is far from unique. If much of high school is relational[84] and we know that social relations differ markedly between and among races, then we can begin to identify one of the key sore spots in the racialization of Prairie Heights.

What I saw at Prairie Heights was a reconfiguration of the school's racial map. Long a school divided into two, stark racial categories, Prairie Heights has had to adjust to many demographic changes, including an ongoing influx of Latino students that has redrawn the racial dividing lines. Race is still a key sorting mechanism at Prairie Heights, though it no longer results in a black-white binary, but rather a far more layered racial hierarchy. While Latino students still face many racial obstacles, they are somewhat privileged vis-à-vis their African-American peers.

---

[84] A student teacher at another high school in Lakeview noted that she had mastered her content area, had a 'toolbox' full of teaching ideas and techniques and got to the classroom only to find that "It's all relational, that's the most important thing in high school."

Chapter 4

Borderlines and Border Crossings: Belonging and Legal Status at School

"During high school, I was an observer at school. I had to learn English, and I had to figure out how to fit into American culture. I had to teach myself how to live in two, very different worlds." Adela, commenting in her college application essay on the difficulties of living a "double life".

Though the students in room 134 are at a great physical distance from the border, in this chapter I argue that the border nonetheless continues to define their lives and their potential for school success. The border profoundly shapes each of those students, as well as greatly affecting the degree to which students are afforded full entry into the school and larger communities. Central to the issue of belonging is their legal status, a key factor in many of the decisions the students make and the ways in which they understand their options. An important gender difference among the students in room 134 is that the boys were more susceptible to a certain kind of peer pressure that enforces a rigid sense of what it means to "be" Latino. For their part, some of the Latinas were able to excel in ways that eluded most of their male counterparts; others were more restricted in their possibilities than their male counterparts and seemed virtually invisible in the eyes of the school.

As immigrant students and their families begin to negotiate the school system after they arrive in the US, they often face serious conflicts about whether or not and *how* to keep their linguistic and cultural identities intact. As Olsen (1997) and other scholars have pointed out, academic success for both immigrant students and for other students who are or *become* the other, is often linked to how successfully students are able to assume an identity as 'American'. This chapter will explore the way in which a sense of true belonging or 'citizenship' is beyond the reach of many of the students in room 134. As previously discussed, becoming 'American' can too often mean giving up something else. There is a long history of immigrant assimilation into US culture and of those who have overtly resisted attempts to be molded into 'real Americans.' That resistance requires not just the maintenance of psychic borders which protect from the daily incursion of mainstream culture, but the constant re-building of those borders in ever more creative ways. The process is further complicated by the current contentious and highly politicized battle over immigration and who is allowed into the fold as a 'real American.' In spite of the public schools' mandate to include all students and the fact that many teachers are wholly committed to that, the battleground has spilled into the hallways of schools like Prairie Heights, with deeply felt consequences for many of the students in room 134. While much has been written about Latino immigrant children, scant light has been shed on the particularities of immigrant children in the upper Midwest. While my interviewees do not live in or occupy a border area, in geographic terms they reside in and are limited by the very real borderlands that have grown up around the immigrant communities in this area, which are traditionally more homogenous than the oft-studied coasts, the Southwest and the southern borderlands.[85]

Student identity and success in high school is in no small way linked to belonging. For my purposes, the concept of a school-based citizenship is useful. Though students can physically enter a school building and enroll in classes, a sense of authentically belonging to that community is often out of reach. As I spent more time in room 134, I realized that full, school-based citizenship was effectively blocked by

---

[85] As Palestinian youth have eloquently put it, they are 'occupied' by the very fact of the border and the way it is used against them.

the reality of the US-Mexican border. That border defined the students' lives to a surprising degree, given its distance and the fact that its reality is barely recognized by many at Prairie Heights and in the surrounding Lakeview community. They don't think about it, simply because they don't have to.[86]   The room 134 students have parents who valued education and 'got' why school was so important; yet the parents are not often listened to or heard within the schools; additionally, they are often incredibly busy, working more than full-time at jobs that may not let them take off an hour in the middle of the day to go see about something at school. Another complicating factor is that many of the parents have not mastered English and may feel uncertain about contacting the school. I had the chance to interact informally with several of these parents at the soccer games I attended to watch some of the 134 boys play. One Prairie Heights' parent from Spain[87] related how her son had been "wasting his time" at a local middle school in math classes several grade levels too easy because he was learning English. This woman speaks English, is affiliated with the university and is herself highly educated, and therefore the school essentially had no option but to listen to her. There are undoubtedly scores of similar cases, but when the parents do not speak English, have little education themselves, are not white and are not comfortable negotiating the school system, they too often end up remaining voiceless. School-based citizenship, then, works not only at the level of the students themselves, but applies to the families and larger communities as well.

The students spoke without exception about the tremendous sacrifice their parents had made to come to the US. "My mom is like

---

[86] Several teachers, and guidance counselors, expressed initial surprise when they realized how daunting a college application and many other official documents could be; one of the first things to be filled out was a student's social security number. That stopped many of the room 134 students dead in their tracks and teachers were not necessarily aware of that.

[87] There is a noticeable difference here; those ELLs who come from Europe or particular Asian countries and have more financial and educational resources at home are granted more status than their Latino counterparts.

my hero", Adela told me. "She works so hard, *so* hard, two jobs, just to make sure we do good. Good in school, and in everything." Adela's father was long gone, leaving her mother the burden of raising the two children, and two jobs that meant she had scant time to help Adela or her brother, Ricardo, with school. Despite their circumstances, by the time I met them, they had long surpassed their mother's level of schooling. Adela was able to do quite well academically, while her brother had a more difficult time. While students like Adela recognized and honored their parents' struggles and cultures, those home cultures are often marginalized or even completely 'disappeared'[88] from the school setting. Because the home culture is not considered legitimate or academic, it is disregarded and replaced. This sometimes happens even with the best of intentions; while teachers or staff members may think that the Spanish language or a student's history or cultural traditions are important, they are seen as linked exclusively to home, rather than to the school environment. "That's not our job," one teacher told me, as we chatted one day about whether or not schools should consider teaching more Mexican history or culture, adding that, "they should be learning that at home." Moll (2001) has done a great deal of relevant work on what he calls 'funds of knowledge' and how imperative it is acknowledge the existing cultural wealth in a given community. Acknowledging the cultural wealth of a community can both spark and deepen each individual student's sense of pride. If culture is key, then teachers of Spanish speaking and other language speaking students as those in room 134 must be prepared to deal with more than just linguistic issues. When children are not allowed to succeed in school unless they assume a new identity, they will continue to be invisible within the larger school context. Schools in Lakeview and around the country are addressing this issue as they pilot bilingual and/or dual immersion programs; to date those have only

---

[88] I use this term, so laden with meaning in Latin America, quite deliberately. It was used initially to refer to actual people who 'disappeared' and presumed dead by the various dictatorships that populated the political landscape of the 1960-'70s. Under the crushing weight of neoliberal economic policies, it has now gained currency to refer to the disappearance of ideas, and even of hope itself.

served a small percentage of elementary school students. In at least one district near Lakeview, a Spanish-English language program touched off a great deal of resistance in the community; in the end the program was shelved in favor of, as one teacher remarked, a "less offensive" second language, in spite of the fact that native Spanish speakers numbered more than 10% of the district's population. This seems to support the trend that the kinds of issues one routinely sees at Prairie Heights will likely persist.

Even as many students are able to master basic English, they often remain confused about the way to *do* things in school—in other words, how to master the discourse of school culture. There are real differences between learning and mastering English, and learning and mastering the discourse of school culture; the latter is essential for real academic success, but it is rarely taught in any explicit fashion, and thus the inequalities with which students enter school only deepen as their schooling continues. Sometimes students who have a fairly high level of academic English run into problems, because of their accents or, some would argue, because of their physical appearance. Luis talked about not feeling entirely comfortable when speaking English. "It pisses me off that you are treated differently, because of how you might talk, because you see that they don't really interact with those who don't speak English well."[89] In fact, his English is fine, though his accent is fairly pronounced and seems to be influential in others deciding that it is not worth the trouble to listen to him.

CITIZENSHIP AND BELONGING

The process which immigrant students go through in the school setting highlights the importance of citizenship. In order for immigrant students to really become 'American' they must leave behind both their culture and their language, and, all too often, their racial identity. For too many public school students becoming American is equivalent to becoming white. As previously mentioned, the students of room 134 routinely referred to the white students as "*americanos,*" while the African-American students were classified by their color. After

---

[89]"Me enojo que el trato no es lo mismo, por como habla uno, por como se ven como que no se interactuan con los que no hablan bien el inglés."

arriving in the US and as they begin to negotiate the school system, immigrant students often face serious conflicts about whether or not and how, to keep their linguistic and cultural identities intact; at the same time, many African American students face the same conflicts and challenges. We see that academic success for immigrant students (as well as for the so-called *other* students - those who are, or become the *other,* most often because of race), is often linked to how successfully students are able to assume an identity as 'American'. This issue of Americanization becomes quite polemical in the current context of increasing Mexican immigration and how that is constructed in the popular imagination.   Mexican immigration has long been absolutely vital to the US economy, and US-government programs bringing in workers over the years (most notoriously, through the *Bracero* program), have promoted immigration, though the border is quick to close down when the US needs change.   Discrimination against both Mexican immigrants and Mexican-Americans, many of whom do not speak Spanish and have never been to Mexico, has a long history in the Southwest, California and Texas (Acuña, 1981; Montejano, 1987).   As Limón (2001) would have it, *Greater Mexico* now symbolically not only reoccupies the lost territory of Mexico, but expands far beyond those mid 19th-century borders, and there is an increasing discomfort regarding this immigrant 'other' from Mexico.[90] The physical border is far more palpable than in years past, with a huge militarized presence along key stretches.   Yet what the US is trying to keep out, with particular ferocity of late, is already here.

At Prairie Heights I saw a regrouping as both the larger Lakeview community and the school community at Prairie Heights shifted to accommodate the new Latino students.   As in many other areas in the country, the Latino population is essential and has kept a certain sector of the economy (the most menial jobs in the service sector, including

---

[90] It is interesting to note how immigrants in the US are most often portrayed as people of color.   Though Russian immigrants make up a huge proportion of the undocumented workers in Chicago, for instance, the INS sweeps at factories and workplaces there focus on those who "look" Mexican.

custodial and kitchen work) going.[91] With every economic contraction, however, varying degrees of hostility and resentment surface, making those workers more vulnerable, and more likely to put up with difficulties at the workplace. Most of the boys in room 134 divided their time between school and work, with some of them putting in more hours at work than a full week's worth of school. While it was a great source of pride for them to be able to contribute to their family's income, they also lamented the fact that they missed out on other things. Few, however, mentioned school-related activities, although all of them mentioned soccer, referring either to informal pick-up play or to the local Latino youth league. Emilio seemed resigned to the fact that school was a stopping-off point for him. "Miss," he said one day, "Someday I'm going to be able to study, to have more of a future. But for now, for me, school isn't helping me that much."[92]

Many schools today acknowledge the existence of 'different' groupings - race or religion for example - but clearly locate those 'different' groups at a pronounced disadvantage vis-à-vis the normative group that defines and regulates school culture. Yuval-Davis (1997) speaks eloquently about citizenship and, while she refers to citizenship in the particular context of a state, her thinking is relevant to the school setting. She looks at citizenship as "an overall concept which sums up the *relationship* between the individual and the state" (my emphasis) (Yuval-Davis, 1997, p. 86). If we substitute "school" for "state" in this instance, we can begin to hammer out a working definition for use in the school context. Yuval-Davis also discusses how the concept of citizenship has been applied very differentially to different people; again, in the school setting, this is highly relevant. There is a long history of immigrant assimilation into US culture and also of those who have overtly resisted attempts to be molded into 'real Americans.' That resistance requires not just the maintenance of psychic borders which protect them from the daily incursion of mainstream culture, but the constant re-building of those borders in ever more creative ways. Any

---

[91] In many areas in the upper Midwest, Latino laborers are essential to the ongoing operation of dairy farms and many other agricultural enterprises.

[92] "Un día voy a poder estudiar, y tener más futuro. Pero ahora, para mi, el colegio no me ayuda mucho."

discussion of belonging or citizenship must take into account the context within which the school functions. Not only do schools both reflect and represent the community, but school administrations function as mini-states, almost always ideologically in tandem with the larger community, yet in some ways far more powerful in terms of their tremendous and thorough-going impact on the daily lives of students.

When I began this study, the debate around immigration, while ongoing, was very much on the political backburner. Though immigrant students had begun to dramatically change the make-up of schools in areas all over the upper Midwest, and were the focus of discussions and concerns in terms of curriculum, teacher hires, etc. in the school setting, those discussions were largely absent in other societal and political arenas. Indeed, my initial understanding of my students looked at them somewhat exclusively in terms of their individual identities, and in the larger context of racial and linguistic policies and politics. Over the course of my research, however, my conversations with the students led me to identify a critical third piece that involves issues of citizenship and belonging. We know how fundamental it is to have a sense of belonging to a school community to achieve academic success. One key issue is the way in which Latino immigrant students have often been understood *only* as language learners, thus masking the many and variegated realities that they both constitute and confront on a daily basis. Language and immigrant student status function as crucial elements in granting or denying students full status as members of their school community and, I argue, as citizens in a far broader sense.

For the Latino students in room 134, there was a far more concrete reality that has to do with the degree to education and other opportunities are accessible to them after high school. What is at stake is the possibility of actually *belonging.* That is the pressing, and now more politically charged than ever, reality of immigration papers and who has or has not legal documents to be present in the United States. Perhaps just as critical as legal status for these students is the way in which the geographical and political reality of the border has created a sort of 'shadow zone' that they occupy both as students and in the everyday world as well. The very existence of the border, and its ongoing weight in these students' daily lives has structured a sort of wall around their lives; while there is admittedly a great deal of flexibility and even the possibility for reaching much potential, that potential is greatly constricted and thus their identity thwarted to a degree. In many ways, one could say that these students are attempting to forge an identity that both recognizes and honors the fact that they have a foot in both worlds, and yet to a great extent, their school experiences deny that very reality.

LOS AMERICANOS

As a small university city, Lakeview has a strong sense of itself as an open, fairly tolerant town. However, some episodes in the city's not so distant past, as well as some fairly recent experiences, would indicate otherwise. The city passed fair housing legislation in 1965, but continues to face charges that its low income housing, a long functioning code for race, has been heavily concentrated in small, relatively ghettoized, areas, and does not begin to meet the needs of the population for which low income housing is the sole option. The city was declared to be out of compliance with desegregation legislation in 1980 and is still in the throes of the court-mandated school desegregation process. After an influx of Latino immigrants, along with significant increases in the African-American and Southeast Asian populations in the schools, White flight accelerated at many schools throughout Lakeview. According to local education blogs and PTA listserves, the white families who left the public schools for other districts, or for parochial and private schools in town would largely refute the label of "white flight"; instead they might phrase their concern about how their children fare in the district using the language of "talented and gifted" (a race-specific code word in the Lakeview district) or argue that their children are not being well served given the many new 'pressures' on the district.[93]

With the exception of one student, all of the students I interviewed were immigrants and all but three were from Mexico. This clearly

---

[93] Mounting budget cuts, paralleled by the significant increases in students from lower SES households, as well as those identified as English language learners, continue to complicate the local debates around education and have ended up with some groups of parents looking to relatively 'easy' targets, i.e. the less connected parents/families, to blame for a school structure that many realize is failing large numbers of students.

played an enormous role in the way they understood themselves in the school setting and, perhaps just as importantly, how the school staff and larger community understood and categorized them. As I spoke with students and the political issues of the day percolated to the foreground in their informal discussions, I realized that not only were the students immigrants, they were almost all undocumented as well.

Though Ms. Lawrence did not necessarily plan or predict this, the very decision to create her class for native Spanish speakers ended up embedding the issue of belonging into the more mundane language discussions from the very beginning. She clearly understood and fought to maintain this space so essential to her students. The class, unfortunately, was canceled for a year and Ms Lawrence was told that it was due to scant enrollment. When she questioned that, she found out that the class was not even offered to students (and was not listed as an elective on the paperwork students received). She was able to get the class reinstated for the following year and continues to teach it. It was striking to me that room 134 functioned as a safe haven of sorts and Ms. Lawrence was clearly beginning to understand it as such. The students were participants in co-creating that sense of safe space, and the issue of "belonging" was embedded from the very beginning. In fact, during my first year with the students, they talked frequently about 'belonging,' whose school this was, and where they might fit in. Carmen spoke more than once about how she felt that many people in the community and at Prairie Heights itself seemed to look at her and the other Mexicans.[94] "They think we are nothing," she said to me one day; she had come into class a bit late and was more than a little upset because she felt a teacher had not treated her respectfully. Then she said something that was to stay with me, pulling me into the day-to-day reality of the students at the micro level of Prairie Heights even as it illuminated the larger context in which their lives played out. "They are going to know how important we are, and they're going to need us.

---

[94] She did say "Mexicans," and had a clear and distinct sense of her own Mexican identity as something to protect against the culture in which she found herself immersed. I found out that she later became a key member of one of Lakeview's Mexican gangs, spending much time and energy engaged in internecine fights with other Mexican youths.

Without Latinos, Americans are nothing, nobody."[95] Carmen's parents both worked long hours, two of the many and often invisible workers who were keeping Lakeview's dishes clean and floors sparkling. Carmen was one of the least engaged students in the class, barely making it in school and not particularly sophisticated about things academic; however, she clearly had a visceral understanding of herself, and many of her peers, as caught in a world that was not only difficult to navigate, but also one that was a virtual minefield of stereotypes imposed from the outside. She touched on what many other students noted only tangentially, openly defending herself and her Latino peers against what she felt to be a generalized feeling in the Prairie Heights and Lakeview communities. "They need to know that they need us, that we are people, that we're not criminals."[96] While the students don't necessarily live it as such, they are cognizant that the outside world sees (or more to the point, doesn't see) them as living in the 'shadowlands.'

As I spoke with the students about their daily lives, most of them talked about how busy they were. All of the boys worked for pay outside the home. Most of the girls had serious, and time-consuming, responsibilities at home; they often referred to time they spent cooking, cleaning or taking care of younger siblings. The students generally attended one of the Spanish-language churches in town, and many mentioned soccer as well as dances at area supper clubs featuring Mexican bands as prime free-time activities. There was a strong sense that they weren't necessarily as 'hooked in' to the traditional school activities such as dances and sporting events as many of their peers. For instance, Emilio lamented the fact that he had to race out as the final bell rang at the school. He explained that he had to catch a bus to the local restaurant where he washed dishes for 5 or 6 hours a night, adding, "No puedo quedarme nunca a hablar con mis amigos." [I can never hang around to talk with my friends.] He quickly noted with pride that he gave "a lot" of money to his mother with each paycheck.

---

[95] "Van a saber que tan importante somos nosotros, y que nos van a necesitar. Sin los latinos, los americanos no son nada ni nadien [sic]."

[96] "Que sepan que ellos necesitan a nosotros, y que somos gente, no somos criminales."

If we understand each school as a community, we can begin to also see that some students have full membership, citizenship, in that community, while others are denied complete access. I have talked about the ways in which race informs and often constricts the daily lives of the Latino students at Prairie Heights, and that is clearly an element that cannot be factored out of our discussion of issues of 'belonging'; however, the element of legal status and citizenship is just as critically important.

Language for many of these students became an important marker of 'belonging,' often in ways that were sophisticated in the sense that they underscored, and perhaps unintentionally strengthened, the faultlines of separation between the Spanish-speaking students and their English-speaking, and particularly their White, peers. On one hand, not speaking English well made it hard for them to forge social links with their peers, even as it often ended up undermining their potential for academic success. Other students, teachers and staff used the fact that the students continued to speak Spanish as a way to identify these students as separate in a negative way from the 'real' school[97]. Language underscored their 'difference,' and became a way for school members to assert their own clear exclusive sense of ownership and citizenship in the larger school community. It was apparent from my interviews that the ones at school who were seen as *really* belonging were, overwhelming, the White students. This is not to say that students of color, especially a number of African-American students, were not popular or well-liked; many were, yet there was a shared, understood sense that even most of those kids were having a tough time getting through the key academic hoops they would need to ensure academic success and, somehow, "full participation", or citizenship, in the school culture. However, in many ways, the Spanish-speaking students are *not* allowed entrance even into the non-academic school community as full citizens.

---

[97] Here again, the classic deficit framework became the default lens through which many teachers/staff *see* those students who have not mastered academic English.

A STAKE IN SCHOOL

Citizenship in the context of Prairie Heights became an increasingly difficult and complicated reality to negotiate for many students. At first glance the factors seemed linked primarily, if not exclusively, to both race and language; they also turn out to have important class components as well. There is a small, but significant, group of 'mixed' or biracial[98] students who tend to have fairly high prestige at the school. Many of them excel either in sports, music or the fine arts, and most of them tend to be fairly good students in terms of their grades. The majority also come from families where at least one or both of the parents is a professional, and often is linked to the nearby university; so the children are accustomed to fairly easy sailing through school, not in terms of the work per se, but in the sense that they know the ropes and are treated as students with much potential. In short, they are granted a measure of citizenship by arbiters of the school system and that makes their experience at school quite different.

It is important to underscore as well that the students in room 134 are quite social and involved in many networks. They are active in many things outside school, as noted, and like any high school student, are tied quite closely into their friends' lives. The picture then, is not one of a brutally segregated high school environment which wholly blocks certain students from success or access to the activities that can make school both enjoyable and fulfilling. Rather, it is an invisible, yet highly stratified screen that sharply limits students' access to the traditional channels of power and achievement within the school context. In many ways, these students struck me as bearing both the burden and, potentially, enjoying the privilege of having a foot in each of two worlds;[99] if we see it exclusively in negative terms, they are caught between two worlds and end up on some profound psychic or linguistic level at times, not fully belonging to either. The potentially positive aspects of being able to move relatively seamlessly between two cultures are something that the school could more actively facilitate, yet many of its actions do just the opposite. My research led

---

[98] Both words that the students themselves use.

[99] How can educators understand this as opportunity, rather than deficit?

me to understand that one of the most salient factors in the lives of these Latino students is in fact, their immigrant status -- a status that continues to be tenuous. While it does not constantly affect daily lives, it is both an ever-present factor in their daily lived reality, as well as an enormous and often insurmountable obstacle as they begin to think about post-secondary education.   This status, combined with the frequent lack of proper guidance, condemns the students to scant academic success, in turn often translating into a lack of any real opportunities.   This was brought home to me one day when Emilio mentioned the many, many hours he worked washing dishes after school. I asked him what time that left him to study, and wondered how he'd be ready for college or technical school after high school. "A mi no me van a aceptar en todo caso." ["Well, they're not going to accept me, anyways."] he said, referring somewhat obliquely to his immigration status, and indicating that this job was the best he thought he could do.

One of the most engaging and consistently 'on' students in the classroom during my first research year was Ricardo.   He was one of the few in that particular class who was quite comfortable with both English and Spanish. He had a clear sense of the larger world outside the school building, but didn't seem entirely sure how to access it.[100] I was surprised to hear from Ms. Lawrence that he almost never attended his other classes, a common phenomenon for many students who showed up fairly regularly in room 134. I heard her point this out to those students more than once, and her warnings were met with sheepish acknowledgement, promises to stop skipping other classes, as well as spot-on critiques of the teachers whose classes they were missing. Perhaps not surprisingly, the promises to shape up were rarely fulfilled.

Ms. Lawrence kept after Ricardo whenever she saw him, trying to get him to attend his other classes and turn in the homework for her class, something he rarely did. Clearly, school was not doing much for him. He worked at a local fast food restaurant, and by senior year, had moved up to assistant manager. Like each of the students I interviewed, he was trying to negotiate an identity authentically *his*; his deep, strong

---

[100] Interestingly, and to his credit, he was the only one who asked me, "How will your study help *us?*"

Mexican roots were extremely important to him, but he noted more than once that he was probably no longer "Mexican enough" to easily fit in with his cousins and other relatives back in Mexico; this topic came up repeatedly as students discussed relatives, all young adults working in areas relatively near the US-Mexican border, who had been deported, some after living since early childhood in the US. Thus, we can argue that the border had effectively *crossed* Ricardo's life, clearly delineating both possibilities as well as impossibilities. Ricardo had a clear grasp of the fragility of his legal situation, as well as a realistic apprehension of the fact that his situation will be even more tenuous once he leaves high school. Though he had a certain sophistication about his own situation, his knowledge was not channeled into any long term political action.[101]

Emilio, along with several of the other boys who were dealing with the fact that they had never mastered Spanish literacy and were now adrift in both English and Spanish, exemplified what seemed to happen to the boys who had made the move to the US when they were either pre-adolescents or teenagers. They never really fit into school, and the school wasn't always sure what to do with them,[102] even though it is legally bound to teach them, and so they ended up in a sort of nether category. As mentioned, Emilio was one of a number of boys who went to work every day after school, working long hours in the kitchens of Lakeview's downtown restaurants. Because of their immigrant status and lack of papers, they were often understood as nothing more than low-wage workers and to some degree they understood themselves that way as well. Many of them had clear and sophisticated analyses of their (both their parents and themselves) role in the labor force, but at

---

[101] After publicly supporting the rights of undocumented students and their families, several staff members in the Lakeview district reported being told, in no uncertain terms that they were not to take a 'political' stance on what they consider to be a human rights issue. One felt pressured to the point where she resigned her position with the district.

[102] A guidance counselor at another local high school has talked in many public forums about the problems he has faced when he insists that the district honor the law and provide education to students, even those who have passed age 18.

times it seemed as if the odds were just too overwhelming. Emilio talked about it this way: "yo no soy para estudiar" ["I'm not much for studying"], adding that making a living was both more important to him at the moment and something he felt he was good at. Projecting into a hypothetical future that hinged on getting through overwhelming academic, financial and legal hoops to continue studying simply didn't seem that important or rewarding when his family's current stability depended in part on him, and so studying simply didn't seem that useful. His decision not to take school very seriously thus made quite a bit of sense, though some teachers were frustrated, and sometimes quick to criticize, as they thought he should 'stick with school.' The fact that high school is hard for a number of the Latino students, and not because of a lack of intelligence, was underscored when a young Latina woman lushly congratulated one of Ms. Lawrence's students who graduated; "the truth is we just don't see many of our *muchachos* making it," she said.

The few boys who managed to 'escape' this fate of many of the Latino boys at Prairie Heights were able to do so primarily because of a link to a particular teacher and/or academic group who believed in them and helped them to negotiate the intricacies and confusing realities of school and post-secondary options. Emilio had a clear allegiance to his Mexican roots and identity, and because of his scant mastery of English, also had a very difficult time crossing boundaries to make friends outside his small Mexican, mostly male group. He seemed to be one of the most disenchanted with school in general and though he came to the Spanish class regularly, he rarely completed his work. He almost never attended his other classes and was failing every one of them. When asked why, he was articulate as he described how he felt about school, and, how school made him feel. "Most of the teachers don't know me well," he said, "it seems like they think I'm sort of stupid."[103] Why did he think that was? "Well, the truth is that I don't go to class a lot of times, maybe it's my fault, right?," he answered, but it's like they think that I can't do anything. Maybe they just think that

---

[103]"La mayoría de los maestros no me conocen bien, parece que creen que soy algo dundo."

Mexicans are dumb?"[104] I asked him why he continued to show up to his Spanish class. "Well, I like being there, I like the teacher, and I like to hang out with everybody."[105] In short, it was the one place in school with the important exception of the "illicit" soccer games[106] where he felt at home, where he felt that he *belonged.*

Because they were integrated or assimilated in ways that Emilio was not, many of the other boys fared somewhat better at school; again, having some sort of connection was essential. Oscar had received a high school 'scholarship' that specifically targeted Latino students as they were entering high school; one or two were chosen annually from Lakeview's dozen-plus middle schools. He had an 'easier' time than most of his peers, but some of the key issues he dealt with were largely beyond the school's ability to cope with. He had a very stable and supportive family, but was expected to do a great deal of work at home with his younger siblings as both of his parents worked more than full-time in menial jobs. Their clear hope was that he would make it to college, the first on either side of his family, and he took that quite seriously. Yet this also caused him problems with some of his peers. He clearly saw himself as a role model for his younger siblings and though that created enormous pressure on him on a day-to-day basis, it was a remarkably positive, if sometimes overwhelming, force.

Domingo had a scholarship similar to Oscar's, which included a computer his freshman year and rather loose monitoring thereafter by the program's administration. He was far shyer and less of a social

---

[104] "Pues, la verdad es que muchas veces no voy a clase, quizás es mi culpa, no? Pero es como creen que no puedo hacer nada, será que piensan que los mexicanos somos tontos?"

[105] "Es que me cae bien estar allí, me cae bien la maestra, y me gusta estar con la gente."

[106] When the weather was nice, many of the Latino boys routinely missed an hour or two of class a day, the class periods directly after their lunch hour; they could almost always be found outside on a small practice field playing intense games of soccer, with no adults in sight. As Emilio once said, "It's the only time we get to play all day," referring to the fact that he and most of the other boys left school to go directly to their jobs, where they might be until 9 or 10 at night.

force than Oscar and seemed to move anonymously through most of his classes. When I interviewed him, he was a senior and had already missed the all-important application deadlines for the local community college and state university. Even with a program ostensibly backing him up, he had fallen through the cracks. Victor was a force of nature, in many ways, socially very adept and clearly quite intelligent. While he did note that a teacher or two was on his side, his prevailing sense was that teachers simply did not pay much attention to him. He was looking for support and recognition and it just didn't seem to be coming from the school. He complained often about school and seemed to realize that it just wasn't set up for students like him. He told me several times that he was hoping to be a police officer. "It's something I could really do," he said. "I know how to talk to people."[107] *"Si,"* Javier teased, "Like, *oye wei*[108], you're under arrest." This sent a few of the boys into gales of laughter, but Victor was insistent that he would someday go into police work.

It was simultaneously interesting and depressing to note that the guidance office was never mentioned by the students as a positive touchstone. Ms. Lawrence mentioned several times that the counselor assigned to over 90% of her students was seen by them as an out and out enemy, 'not on our side' as Ricardo put it. The students understood this as linked to the issue of immigration status, as the counselor did not have to deal with the issue of legal status herself; also she consistently seemed to consciously or unconsciously offend her students by assuming things about them that simply were not true.[109] While I give credence to the students' point of view, it is also true that

---

[107] "Es algo que realmente podría hacer, sé como hablar con la gente."

[108] *Guey*, often rendered as *wei,* is Mexican slang, and can be roughly translated as 'man' or 'dude.' It was used frequently in room 134.

[109] While she had mastered the language of high expectations and achievement, more than half of the students insisted that she didn't seem to "understand" or "like" the Latino students. Whether or not it was true, they experienced that to be the case and felt that her lack of understanding was directly related to the fact that she looked down on them because of their lack of legal standing. This seems to underscore the need for schools to exercise caution and essentialize all Latinos into one single type when they are hiring.

most teachers and staff members are greatly overburdened in terms of the numbers of students they are expected to reasonably serve. Class sizes continue to creep up and guidance counselors have seen their caseload increase exponentially over the last decade or so. It is an extremely difficult situation for the teachers and staff, and students across the board are paying the price.

There was a clear gender division among the students in room 134 in terms of their academic performance, if not so much in terms of their dreams (they are all happily inspirational in that way). Most, though not all, of the boys were mediocre students at best in terms of their grades; many of them consistently missed classes and were barely able to eke out passing grades. Not surprisingly, some of these very boys were also articulate and passionate when they spoke about things they were interested in or cared strongly about. Alex, for instance, loved cars and knew how to fix them. I know nothing about cars, but his enthusiasm for the topic was palpable and the conversations we had about his passion were engaging and interesting. For some reason, though, he couldn't be bothered to even sign up for the mechanics classes at school. "Well, it's just that, I don't know, I like to hang out at the garage, I know a lot about fixing cars, but those classes just don't do it for me, who knows why?" [110] Alex was also fairly articulate about political issues, but was not even aware that Prairie Heights offered several classes on current events and social issues. Like Emilio, many of the boys carried huge financial and familial burdens on their shoulders and did so with much grace.

The girls were a somewhat different story, and although this may not at first glance seem to have much to do with immigration status, it in fact is quite closely related. After two years of working with the different classes in room 134, I would describe most of the girls as fitting into three admittedly inspecific categories: those who were highly motivated and more importantly, who had caught the attention of a teacher and were being shepherded through school by that teacher; those girls who fell through the cracks but managed to at least keep afloat (although anecdotal evidence suggests that they actually were not

---

[110] "Es que, yo no sé, a mi me gusta estar en el taller, sé mucho ya sobre reparar carros, pero estas clases, no me atraen, quien sabe por qué."

able to do that all so well); and the girls who became pregnant (five in the classroom over the two years I was there, over 20% of all the girls in those two classes). Initially, I didn't think too much about the pregnant girls as a separate category, until I heard multiple times from different girls who admitted that they had 'decided" to get pregnant because the child would be born in the US, thereby affording *them* legal status as the mothers. I realized that for some of these girls this was an extremely logical decision, made in an attempt to deal definitively with the weight of their legal status; although Homeland Security does not see things that way, it was universally, or in this small corner of the universe, what the girls understood to be true.   So, in the midst of the difficult burdens of legal status, lack of assistance, etc., I also saw much agency on the part of the girls. They are all eminently aware of the issue of the border and their legal status, and are making 'common sense' decisions in that context.[111]   A somewhat similar decision was floated by several of the boys; Javier and Victor both thought that joining the Army would afford them legal residence and, possibly, citizenship. David was dismissive. "Dude, that's only if you die," was his harsh assessment. Ricardo went straight to the point. "Why would you do *that*??" he asked. "It's not *our* war."

Natalia and Adela were two girls who did well. Natalia's two older brothers (whom she allowed "are much smarter than me,") had dropped out of high school long before senior year, feeling simply that they did not fit in and found little motivation at school to succeed. Natalia says that she frequently missed classes, and had a hard time sparking herself to go to school during middle school, though she is clearly a very intelligent young woman. She was pushed to success by Ms. P,[112] crossed borders in her relationships at school, most notably with her White boyfriend, and was able to stay in school and do quite well. Adela was another notable example of a girl who made good, so to speak. Ricardo's younger sister, she was one of the students most at ease with switching between English and Spanish. In the Spanish for Spanish speakers class, students jockeyed to get her as a partner in

---

[111] While to an outsider, getting pregnant may not seem wise, these girls were convinced that it would bring them the legal respite they needed.

[112] See Chapter 6.

paired activities, and often sought her help with fine-tuning their writing. Ms. Lawrence recommended that she take a traditional Spanish class the following year. When she did enroll, Ms. Lawrence mentored her through it, essentially running interference for her, as the class was difficult because of the tension Ms. Lawrence had noted – that the native Spanish speakers had a hard time fitting in the traditional Spanish classes. She felt "weird" when the other students wondered why she didn't simply know everything already; "It's not like *they* know everything in English," she pointed out. Adela did very well in the class, in spite of her repeated complaints about how "lonely" she felt. Ricardo, however, never got on track academically, instead working long hours at a restaurant in Lakeview and contributing a large amount to the monthly rent for the apartment he shared with his mother and Adela. In both Adela's and Natalia's cases, it seemed that, consciously or not, the brothers ended up sacrificing quite a bit so that their sisters could do well.

Camila was a slightly different story. She was the only one in the whole class with papers during my first year in room 134. This only became apparent to me around the time of the immigrant rights march. Her status caused serious schisms in the class and touched off much resentment within room 134, even though she did very well in the larger school context. She was easily the whitest student in the class, and was not from Mexico, something she loudly proclaimed to anyone who lumped her in with the other students as "Mexican". Her immigrant experience was the only one that involved getting on a plane and flying into the US, with all the proper documents in hand. In large part because she had attended schools with very small Latino populations for her elementary and middle school experiences, she was far more assimilated into the mainstream school culture than the other students. She was proud of her Argentinian roots, but also felt more removed from them than some of her Mexican peers did. As she often reminded me, "I'm not Mexican; these guys aren't always that nice to me, you know." She felt more than a little bit on the defensive in the class, though she made friends as the year went on.

While Natalia, Adela and Camila all did fairly well in school for somewhat different reasons, a number of the girls who came through room 134 seriously struggled not only with the class, but with school in general. At least four girls became pregnant during that first school year, including Cerina who had initially seemed to be on the road to at least completing high school. She spoke quite decisively several times in class (after she was already pregnant, as I later realized) about the "fact" that any baby born in the US was a citizen and therefore that baby's mother was also protected. "No te pueden deportar si tienes un bebé gringo" ["They can't deport you if you have a *gringo* baby"], she explained to her classmates. Ms. Lawrence gently pointed out the inaccuracies in her argument, but that did not seem to faze or deter her. While the other girls who became pregnant did not speak as specifically about the issue of legal status, it was a topic that fairly frequently found its way into classroom conversation and it was clear to me that Cerina's beliefs were almost unanimously shared. Cerina and the other pregnant girls left Prairie Heights for a district-wide program geared exclusively towards pregnant girls. She reported that she liked it very much, and said she was hoping to finish school after her baby was born.

THE BORDER CROSSED US

The issue of immigration as a topic of conversation did come up that first year with the students, but it was not a particularly burning issue. Until April. In the late winter and spring of 2006, the immigration issue came to a head in many cities and towns around the country. The struggle for immigrant rights came to a head, in part after Rep. James Sensenbrenner introduced legislation (HR 4337) that would have criminalized those who helped any undocumented persons; the wording was vague enough and mean-spirited enough that it was not a stretch to suppose that even teachers could be held in contempt, simply for teaching students who did not happen to have papers. The resulting debate created a virtual firestorm in Ms. Lawrence's class and several class periods and assignments were dedicated to this subject as she realized the intensity of their interest in the issue; the fact that she took the issue seriously, and gave her students a forum and safe place to discuss it, showed utter respect for, and understanding of, her students. I never asked the students about their immigration status in my one-on-one interviews, however, as they discussed the growing political controversy over immigration in the country, they referred time and again to the fact that most of them did not have legal status. Ms. Lawrence asked me to give them a brief lesson on the history of immigration in the US, to provide the historical context in which to better understand the current situation. Victor already had some insights. "I don't understand this whole problem about immigration here these days, because this country is the way it is because the White people came from Europe. I mean, they are immigrants, too."[113] Hearing this, Oscar added, "It's true; the only thing is that we are the first generation."[114] Perhaps without even knowing it, he was alluding to the long sweep of Mexican immigration in the US, and also distinguishing himself from many generations who came before him. In other parts of the US, while many Mexican students may in fact be *"primera generación"*, or first generation, there is also a significant population of Chicano or Mexican-American students who claim a racial identity distinct from many of their white peers, even as they simultaneously see themselves as American.

Knowing more details of the history of immigration made many of the students feel rather angry and resentful that they had to deal with so many more hoops than previous immigrants to the US. I spoke to them about my grandparents as immigrants and their buy-in to the racial pact. This sparked a series of questions about what they *weren't* learning at school, with Javier leading it off by noting that they had *never* learned Mexican history, even though it is so important to US history.[115] Some of the students complained that the one Latin American history course at the school barely discusses Mexico. "The Americans," Javier complained one day, "don't know anything, they don't know how big Mexico used to be, they don't know why people have to leave and come look for a future here."[116]

---

[113] "No entiendo todo este problema de la inmigración aquí ahora, porque el país se hizo tal como está porque vinieron los blancos de Europa. O sea, son inmigrantes ellos tambien."

[114] "Es cierto … la única cosa es que somos la primera generación."

[115] And, not surprisingly, many of the students did not know much about Mexican history, other than broad strokes. They knew, however, that it was important for them *to* know.

[116] "Los americanos," Javier complained one day, "ni saben nada … no saben lo grande que era Mexico antes, no saben por qué la gente tienen que salir y buscar vida aquí."

As activists in the larger community organized for what would turn out to be a huge march for immigrant rights, many of the students at Prairie Heights also began to organize, as did their peers at other high schools. The two main organizers, both Latino students at Prairie Heights, were students who were on 'safer ground'; both had citizenship, had parents with advanced degrees and stable employment and were recognized by school staff as leaders. They worked with community activists to organize a walkout from Prairie Heights on the day of the march. District policy allowed students to leave only if they filled out a permission slip from their parents, though some teachers decided to have tests that day, complicating the decision for some of the students. The Prairie Heights organizers talked to a number of students in Ms. Lawrence's class and Ricardo, in particular, talked up the march in class. It was clear that it was taken for granted by the students in room 134 that they *all* would be at the march. Ricardo mentioned to me that he felt it might be a little weird to try and organize "the *americanos*" (his term) to walk out. "They might think I'm doing it just for me," he worried, though he felt sure that a lot of the Prairie Heights kids would probably go to the march. "They're cool and all," he said. "I think a lot of them will show, and maybe some just want to get out of school, but a lot of them are into it." Victor's take on it all was simple, and to the point. "Soy latino, y como muchos otros, me gustaría tener una vida mejor." [I'm Latino and, like a lot of other people, I would like to have a better life."] Although he did not have to worry about papers as he had been born in the US, David was vocal in his support of his classmates. "It's fair," he said on more than one occasion. "It's just fair to treat people like human beings. All anyone wants is a better life."

Most of the Latino students did not formally walk out the day of the march. They did not attend school at all that day, in fact, instead heading out to the march from home with their families. It was clear that this was a matter, if not of life and death, then of something that directly and profoundly affected their lives, and those of their families. In conversations with some of the non-Latino kids at school, students' motivations for attending the march ranged from a broad and fairly sophisticated understanding of the issues to a rather inarticulate but well-intentioned sense of justice.

Prairie Heights has a fairly liberal student body, (a student mock presidential election in 2004, two years before the march, had Ralph

Nader running neck and neck with John Kerry, with President Bush garnering less than 5% of the total vote). More than 300 students walked out of Prairie Heights that morning (many others told me that they were afraid, or unable to, because they had tests scheduled) to march the two miles to the main gathering site. Students from other area high schools joined in as well. I was at the march and saw almost of the students from room 134. Many families were there ("a virtual parade of strollers", as one political blog put it), and the mood was festive and hopeful. Domingo may well have summed up what he and his fellow students were feeling the best. "I didn't know there were so many of us", was his half-shouted greeting as he saw me as we were marching up one of Lakeview's wide downtown streets. Victor was exuberant when I ran into him a little later.

The day before the march, he had admitted that he just "didn't understand the big problem with immigration." The sheer numbers (15,000+) of people at the march led to a feeling, more than anything else, of possibility. Carmen, who often seemed disaffected at school, was positively bubbly the day after the march, repeating herself over and over to me. "I went to the immigrant march yesterday, I saw everyone there, people from all the schools, my friends and family."[117]

Controversy was touched off in the class when it became clear that one student, and in fact *only* one, from the entire class had NOT gone to the demonstration. Ms. Lawrence called me the night of the march to let me know that only Camila had attended class that day. She was concerned that Camila might have a hard time with the other students and resolved not to say anything to the others that would reveal that Camila had not gone to the march. As it turned out, Camila essentially 'outed' herself to the class. She laughed nervously as she mentioned she had been at school all day which caused some looks of genuine shock among the other students and an almost immediate sense of palpable tension. "Of course she stayed at school," Javier muttered, "what does it matter to her?"[118] While the tension dissipated by the end of the school year, it did not disappear, and it was fairly evident that

---

[117]"Ayer yo fui a la marcha de los inmigrantes, vi a todos allí, a la gente de todos los colegios, a mis amigos, a mi familia ..."

[118] "Claro que se quedó en el colegio, que le importa a ella?"

many of the other students in room 134 felt that she had in a sense abandoned them.

About a year after the huge demonstration, there was a flurry of immigration roundups in and around Lakeview. I received a phone call one Sunday evening from a local Latino activist notifying me that people were worried that ICE was going to be doing checks at the local schools. The next day, more than 70% of the district's Latino students stayed home. One teacher remarked to me that this was a sad sign indeed, seeing it as an indication that those students had somehow been duped into believing that they were in danger. However, it could also be seen as an indication of the profound connections and networking in the very vibrant Lakeview Latino community that has emerged, as well as of the tremendous separation that community feels from the sources of power and decision-making.[119]   It was also a clear sign that hope was beginning to dissipate.

The march underlined the shifting terrain on which students were attempting to negotiate not only their school selves, but their very lives. Even at this remove, the border turned out to be a formidable obstacle as well as an arbiter of what they could not only do, but even hope for. The students both absorbed and challenged messages they received about Mexico from school, media, and other sources.   When a counselor came to class one day to tell the students about an upcoming event, she jokingly scolded them saying, "Hora americana, not puertoriqueña!" [American time, not Puerto Rican time!] Several of the boys groaned in derision. "Mexico!" Luis shouted out. "Mexico forever!"

Luis and his cousin Alex spent a great deal of time in class trash talking each other, and frequently used anti-Mexican stereotypes in their own bickering. When Luis let a crumpled first draft fall on the floor one day in class, Alex called Ms. Lawrence's attention to it. "*Maestra!*" he called out. "One of those poor Mexicans threw something on the floor again." They were constantly reclaiming and declaring their own identity, demonstrating a strong sense of self-reflection, even as they perhaps inevitably absorbed much of the public

---

[119] It would be important for the Lakeview district to tap into (not exploit) these already existing networks, and as well to learn from them.

sentiment about, and often against, Mexicans and other Latinos. Luis discussed one of his main problems with Lakeview in general as the increasing number of Mexicans in town. "I don't know, it's getting worse, there is more violence ... when I came, there weren't that many Mexicans, there's a lot, that's bad, because there are always problems in the neighborhoods where there are a lot of Mexicans, there's not much unity among them."[120] He, of course, is also Mexican, though as someone who sees himself as a more established immigrant rather than a newcomer, his views are not novel. Many immigrants turn on newer groups of immigrants, even when those immigrants come from the same country, as they may see them as threatening their already tenuous status in the US; this was the case in California in 1994 when some long-established immigrant populations supported the passage of Proposition 187, which prohibited the provision of many services to undocumented immigrants. This collective viewpoint has gained traction at Prairie Heights as more Mexican and Latino students enter the school in a local and national context where their presence is often contested, and negative stereotypes about them abound. David talked quite openly about the stereotypes one day. "If you look at it, though, from both perspectives, I mean here at school most white kids are scared of black and Mexican kids, like they think you're gonna do something, or whatever." Javier jumped in, "So are *you* afraid of Mexicans and black people?" David was both shocked and insulted. "Of course not, I'm *Mexican*. What the f--k, dude?"

The overwhelming majority of the students in room 134 referred (in English) to Mexico as "over there," as if it was anywhere from a few blocks to thousands of miles away. There is a huge and palpable sense of longing that sings out in the words of these students. Many talk about going back, although not all of them have strong personal memories of the country they left as tiny children. When a student well-known to all in room 134 died in an auto accident, the funeral home in Lakeview was replete with images of the *Virgen de Guadalupe*, patron saint of Mexico; the Mexican national flag and the

---

[120] "No sé, se está poniendo peor, más violencia ... cuando llegue no había muchos mexicanos, ya hay muchos, es malo, siempre hay problemas en los vecindarios donde hay muchos, hay poca unidad entre ellos."

flag of the young man's favorite Mexican soccer team. It underscored the ways in which many of the students are part of a vibrant, local community that has absolutely nothing to do with their school lives or identities.

HOLDING CULTURE CLOSE

The march underscored the shifting terrain on which students were attempting to negotiate their school selves and so much more. When I asked them if they thought they might be losing their culture after so many years in the US, the responses were thoughtful and often poignant. Oscar went back and forth between Spanish to English when spoke to me, but ultimately responded in Spanish. "No, sometimes you get here, and you think that you might lose your culture, but the truth is that you carry it inside, you have your culture inside of you, the truth is that there is something, that your culture never leaves you."[121] He talked about how much his parents had done to teach him about the parts of Mexico he simply no longer remembered. He noted with some sadness that his younger siblings had virtually no memories of Mexico, one having been US-born), and he wondered how they would feel at his age. "My little sisters speak English, but I don't like that, not because I don't want them to learn English, but because I don't' want them to lose their Spanish."[122] Oscar clearly sees himself as part of an intermediate generation and bears some of the particular burdens of being 'caught in the middle.' Language is crucially important to how these students see, and understand, their culture. Javier was perhaps more optimistic. "I think it depends on the person, like if you think that if you keep your culture, that they're not going to accept you, and then you change …"[123] He was adamant, however, about the fact that he

---

[121] "No, a veces vienes, y piensas que puedes perder la cultura, pero la verdad es que tú adentro lo llevas, tú tienes tu cultura adentro, la verdad es que hay algo, la cultura nunca se va".

[122] "My little sisters speak English, but I don't like that, not because I don't want them to learn English, but because I don't' want them to lose their Spanish."

[123] "Yo creo que depende en la persona, por si piensas que si sigues con tu cultura, que no te van a aceptar, y cambias... "

identified as Mexican, and specifically linked that back to his mother, who does not speak English and therefore Javier speaks to her in Spanish; he speaks English with his siblings and with his father as well. Victor also identified himself first and foremost as Mexican.

"I know what the culture is, but I haven't practiced it; there's a lot of people who don't even know what their culture is, but I know my culture and where I come from; others don't know what Mexico is about or what the Mexican culture is, there are other indigneous people for example who also come from Mexico, and they speak English, but they know their culture and they practice it; I know mine, but I don't practice it, the fact is that I know where I'm from, no matter where I am, my country will always be there."[124] While Maria acknowledged that "not being born here makes everything more complicated," she is proud of her rich heritage. The fact that she often easily, switches between Spanish and English underscores this and she is more aware than most students her age of what language can mean, if only potentially. As she discusses her culture, she sees her two worlds as positive. "I like it because I know another language, a different kind of knowledge...knowing about another culture is really good."[125]

Students noted that being native speakers of English (one or two of the Latino students did distinguish between "English" and "good English" which, from their experience, was almost solely the province of their white peers) was an essential, if not sole, indicator of power. Many students in room 134 also pointed to mastery of Spanish language as a key element that could to some degree erode the racial barriers at school. As they begin to negotiate the school system after they arrive in the US, immigrant students and their families oftentimes

---

[124] "Yo sé cual es la cultura, pero no lo he practicado; hay mucha gente que ni si quieren saben lo que es su cultura, pero yo sé cual es mi cultura y de donde vengo; otros no saben de que se trata mexico o como es la cultura de mexico hay otros indígenas por ejemplo que tambien vienen de mexico hablan inglés y todo pero si saben de su cultura y lo practican; yo me lo sé, pero no lo practico; si, el hecho de que sé que soy de allí no importa donde esté, mi patria siempre va a estar".

[125] "Me gusta porque sé otra idioma, otra sabiduría ... saber de otra cultura es muy buena."

face serious conflicts about whether or not (as well as how) to keep their linguistic and cultural identities intact. Much Chicano literature, from novels to more theoretical tracts, speaks to the ways in which, historically, many Chicano students have overtly resisted attempts to be molded into 'real Americans.' That resistance requires not just the maintenance of psychic borders which protect them from the daily incursion of mainstream culture, but the constant re-building of those borders in ever more creative ways.

Linked to this issue of becoming 'American' are the larger issues of citizenship around which the entire framework of the public school is constructed. This ongoing struggle over who is granted full citizenship (as others are accorded only partial recognition) can be very detrimental to students' sense of themselves. There is a somewhat insidious way that the ongoing discussions of both equality and diversity, here understood as recognizing and, perhaps, empowering the identities of a wide range of students, can be easily derailed into a fairly simplistic model; in the case of many schools, this ends up reinforcing the existing and harsh inequities that abound in school. In their conversations with me, the students in 134 showed much understanding of what it meant to live in the virtual shadowlands even if they didn't always know what to do with it. The issue of being suspended between two worlds (tightrope walking, as it were) is nothing new in the world of public schools. Yet today's very particular political reality, combined with economically catastrophic conditions, makes it increasingly difficult for these students. They are on the defensive in ways that immigrant students before them were not, and that is in no way to suggest that earlier groups of students had it 'easy.' Yet today's emphasis on legal papers and the very serious consequences students and their families face without that legal basis is very different from the situation that immigrant students in the first half of the 20th century dealt with. They also have the means to stay in touch with their home country, though the physical journeys back and forth (a possibility, often only realized at great expense and sacrifice) have all but dried up. Phone calls and internet communication mean that students can often stay in touch and connect with cousins or grandparents, which is quite an important thing, but can also contribute to the tension of always feeling pulled between worlds. And they still deal with many in the school who simply don't 'get' where they are coming from. Luis told me that if he were the principal at Prairie Heights, "I would treat everyone the same, I don't like that they treat us differently."[126] Adela talked about her experience in an elementary school in California where, she said, "Most of the teachers said I was never going to learn."[127] After Ms. Lawrence invited a well-known Lakeview lawyer, an immigrant, to talk to the class, Adela was intrigued. "I would like to know, as an immigrant; how he was able to be so successful in life…I would like to be successful like that."[128] However, this immigrant lawyer seemed woefully clueless as to how vastly his immigration experience, more than 25 years earlier, differed from that of the young students to whom he was speaking. Ms. Lawrence's attempt to create both a safe space for their use of Spanish, as well as an important academic and knowledge base, is vitally important, but seems in danger of being drowned out by the other demands and curricular strictures of school.[129]

NEGOTIATING THE GULF

The more time I spent in room 134, the more students began to reveal their very precarious legal situations. While it was talked about in very personal terms in conjunction with the march and its larger political implications, perhaps it was most concretely discussed among the very few who had set their sights on some kind of post-secondary education. In the year or two before my time at Prairie Heights, most students had the option to fill out a paper application for the local community college or university. Those applications asked for social security numbers which undocumented students did not have; many students

---

[126] "Trataría a todos iguales, no me gusta que nos tratan diferentes…"

[127] "La mayoría de los maestros decían que yo nunca iba a aprender."

[128] I would like to know, como inmigrante, como el sacó tanto éxito en la vida … es que yo quiero ser exitoso así."

[129] It will be interesting to see what happens to the Lakeview district in the future. With more and more Spanish speaking students in the primary grades, bilingual programs have taken hold and there has been some experimentation with dual immersion programs for both native Spanish speakers and native English speakers. The district has been forced to recast its policy on language learning, though Ms. Lawrence's students never benefited from that.

left that part blank and their applications were still processed. However, as that option closed and electronic applications became the norm, students were faced with the requirement of having to punch in a social security number as one of the very first questions and before they were able to go on to the next question. The lack of a social security number effectively cut huge numbers of students from the pool of potential applicants.

After the march, there was a great sense of hope and a possibility that things *could* change in terms of national immigration policy, and with that change, all that it would mean for students in Lakeview, at Prairie Heights and in Room 134. But that hope had dissipated by the time school started the next year, and the students were increasingly aware of how their legal status severely constricts what they will be able to do as human beings. There was a clear sense of great hope evaporating, as well as a sense of betrayal. Adela was depressed. "We thought that people cared, that *something* would change. I don't believe in anybody anymore." Students like Adela suddenly understood themselves as stranded in a kind of no-man's land.[130] This situation was not created by the schools, yet it deeply affects the way each school's undocumented Latino students see themselves and the degree to which they can become part of the larger school community.

We have seen the tremendous daily impact that the border and the ever present reality of living without legal status have on the students of room 134, and what they understand to be their possibilities and potential. As the study drew to a close, immigrant students all over the country were facing a harsh political backlash that threatened to demonize their very existence.

---

[130] Adela and the others were the quintessential "dreamers", those students who would be benefited by the passage of the DREAM (Development, Relief and Education for Alien Minors) Act.

Chapter 5

Gatekeepers, Language and Lost Opportunity at Prairie Heights

As we have seen, racial faultlines and the reality of the border cut across and greatly inform student experiences at Prairie Heights in terms of identity and legal status. I use the term "gatekeeping" to refer to another lens through which to look at student opportunities. A number of gatekeepers play key roles at Prairie Heights in that they either open or close doors to Latino students. These roles are both institutional and individual; my observations in room 134 showed that institutional roles tend to close doors to students even though this may not be the intention of the school staff involved, while it is individual teachers and staff who go out of their way to open doors and make more opportunities available to students. Prairie Heights also has an almost all white, highly educated, upper middle class, skilled and powerful parent community that advocates for its children, sometimes to the detriment of other students. Language instruction, as well as the way non-native English speakers are understood, is a key element in the ongoing 'gatekeeping.' Knowledge about and access to post-secondary options is another critical area. Students routinely described a situation to me in which it was fairly difficult for them to take full advantage of the opportunities at Prairie Heights and beyond.

As the population of native Spanish speakers in the Lakeview schools continues to grow, the question of *how* to teach these children is the subject of ongoing and often intense, debate. It is a debate that takes place almost exclusively within the bounds of language policy and practice, and thus is stripped of any larger cultural or political context.

Most of the students in room 134 received some level of ESL services at Prairie Heights. David, who was born in the US, and Camila, who came to the US mid-way through elementary school from the Southern Cone, did not receive ESL services, but even several students who had very high levels of English such as Ricardo, Adela and Victor had some ESL support in their classes. This support ranged from having teachers who were certified both as ESL teachers and in their own field to having an aide float in and out of the class.

Adela was of two minds about this assistance. She liked having teachers who "know what to do" with students who are not native English speakers, but was worried that this put her at a disadvantage in the larger scheme of things. "I think that sometimes they think we just aren't smart enough to take the 'real' classes." I asked her what she meant by "real" classes. "You know," she said, "like any math after geometry, the harder science courses, advanced language, any AP classes." It is certainly striking to walk into an AP class at Prairie Heights and see a room full of kids who are overwhelmingly white. Adela was actually ahead of the pack in room 134, as she was taking some of the more traditional college preparatory classes.[131] However, she was not in any of the AP/Honors courses in either math or science, opting only to do AP Spanish after much support and persuasion on Ms. Lawrence's part. So, while she left Prairie Heights with more math and science than a number of her peers, getting on track in college to enter a field that would require some math or science expertise meant "making up" a number of classes that most college bound students are able to take care of in high school.

Most of the other students were far behind in math and science, and not doing particularly well in any of the courses they were taking. When I asked individual students about their level of knowledge in math and/or science, several noted that the most decisive math years are in middle school (some might argue that it's actually earlier), as the middle school 'track' in which students are placed carries on to high school. Almost all of the students in room 134 were still receiving

---

[131] At this writing, Adela and some of her peers are trying to bring attention to what they called a "deliberate" attempt to misinform students about their options in high school which significantly shape what they are able to do once out of high school.

substantial ESL assistance as middle schoolers.   In the Lakeview district, this generally means more basic math options. Most of the parents of the Latino students had tenuous relations with the schools at best and were in no position to effectively advocate for their students. Ultimately, the room 134 students told me, they ended up in traditional or basic middle school math classes, not the 8th algebra or geometry offered to many students as a lead-in to advanced placement/honors courses in high school. Adela did have one potential, if partial, solution to this problem which deserves reflection. "They should teach math in Spanish," she said, "but real math, the *real* stuff."[132]   As Lakeview moves to a model of more bilingual and/or dual language instruction, this may well become part of that new paradigm, and would surely give native Spanish speakers a more equal footing on this important terrain.

Academic achievement continues to be a huge filter at Prairie Heights and this too is a complicated issue. Although Prairie Heights prides itself on being "a school of excellence" and regularly sends many of its students on to prestigious colleges, including a handful of students to Ivy League schools, many of the students of color are shut out of the mix early on in their high school careers. Anecdotally, I heard from many students and teachers who seemed to blame the students of color for their lack of success in high school. They were implicitly (and sometimes explicitly) described as lazy, unmotivated, not willing to do the work they needed to do and, frighteningly often, as just not smart enough to cut it.   Often, their families and family dynamics were brought into the mix, and pointed to as the primary cause for their lack of success.

Language is an important marker of 'belonging' for the students in room 134, in ways that were often sophisticated; the students underscored that even as, however unintentionally, they strengthened the faultlines of separation between the Spanish-speaking students and their English-speaking peers, particularly the white ones.   On the one hand, not speaking English well made it hard for them to forge social links with their peers, and it often ended up undermining their potential

---

[132] As a college student, Adela realizes more concretely the degree to which her options were shaped by her high school experience. She said to me, "F--k the system … this is why more of *us* need to become teachers."

for academic success. Other students as well as teachers and staff, negatively used the fact that the students continued to speak Spanish as a way to identify these students as separate from the 'real' school.[133] Language underscored their 'difference,' and became a way for school members to assert their own clear and clearly, exclusive sense of ownership/citizenship in the larger school community. My interviews clarified that the ones at school who were seen as *really* belonging were, overwhelming, the white students. This is not to say that students of color, especially a number of African-American students, were not popular or well-liked, many were; yet there was a shared, understood sense that even most of those kids were having a tough time getting through the key academic hoops they would need to ensure academic success and 'full participation' (citizenship) in the school culture. However, in many ways, even as full citizens, the poorer Spanish-speaking students simply do not have access as full citizens, even to the non-academic arenas of the school community. According to the students, part of the problem is that *"los blancos"* don't really want large numbers of other students to get involved in a given activity. Once again, the issues of soccer and, to a lesser degree, social events such as school dances came up. A number of students also pointed to particular structural barriers they face because of the hours they must work (either at home, or in a low-paying job, usually washing dishes – sometimes for upwards of 30 hours each week) to help their families. Emilio put it this way, "Well, the immigrants, and the minorities, it's really hard, a lot of them have to work and their families have to work a lot and that affects them in everything in school."[134]

Though Lakeview schools in general and Prairie Heights in particular do not officially track their students, in practice we see that two students in the very same school can have vastly different experiences. For college-bound students, there is a highly challenging, rigorous course of study that prepares students well for even the most

---

[133] Here again, the classic deficit framework became the default lens through which many teachers/staff *see* those students who have not mastered academic English.

[134] "Bueno, los inmigrantes, y los minorías, es muy difícil, muchos tienen que trabajar y sus familias tienen que trabajar mucho y eso les afecta en todo en el colegio."

difficult of post-secondary options. For others, however, the school provides at best an average education. Much of the rub lies in who makes the decisions about which students are college bound. Counselors have considerable power in that they are often the ones who help channel students toward 'extra' help including summer programs and leadership opportunities, and they can open a number of doors for those students.

Room 134 students Oscar and Domingo were selected as 8th graders as part of an exclusive program to help ensure success for Latino students throughout high school and beyond. That program provided them with some sporadic mentoring in high school, and extra help for post-secondary planning.   However, the person in charge of the program worked for all the Lakeview schools, not only Prairie Heights, and she had a huge amount on her plate; it was hard, if not impossible, for her to keep on top of an ever increasing group of kids. Domingo, for instance, was almost completely unaware of key technical school and college application deadlines and even less aware of possibilities for aid or assistance. The students who were not part of this program were entirely n their own. When I mentioned this to a white, middle-class parent of a Prairie Heights student, she argued that her daughter had not received much help from *her* counselor over the years.   While I do not dispute her assessment of the situation, this actually underscores one way in which many students are at a disadvantage, a disadvantage that is particularly difficult for Latino immigrant students to overcome.

One consistent factor that came up in a number of my interviews with the students was the role of the school guidance counselors. The racial politics I describe must, of course, be contextualized within the larger political and economic forces buffeting school systems across the country and taking an enormous toll on individual teachers and staff members. Since the early 1990s, the budget for Lakeview schools has taken hit after hit, and cuts have gone far beyond the proverbial fat and deep into the bone of schools across the district. One consequence of the ongoing budget cuts (referred to by one teacher as a 'scorched earth' policy) is that teachers and staff alike are dealing with hugely increased class sizes and/or caseloads.   I am mindful of the many stresses that teachers and staff face, the truly crushing pressure put on them, and the increasingly complex problems that their students must deal with. Counselors often end up spending vast amounts of time (and rightfully so) with students in crisis, and may be left with scant time for the other students.

Yet, many of the students from Room 134 reported that they did not feel that their counselors 'believed" in them, or thought that they could 'make it' beyond high school. From the students' perspective, they were seen as less competent students and many of them felt that the counselors were not there to support them, or push them forward. There were a few Latino counselors at Prairie Heights over a period of some 10 years; significantly, all had been born and raised in the US and all had legal documents, and not one had any Mexican heritage. The students perceived that the Latino counselors were not any more likely to understand or help them than a non-Latino counselor; in fact there was a great deal of antipathy against one of the counselors who, according to Javier, "hates us 'cause we're Mexican." I have no way of assessing the veracity of that charge, but it was clear to me that students understood their racial identities and legal status as affecting the way key school authorities perceived them. Witnessing several distinct moments when the counselor came to room 134 was sobering. The students almost immediately shut down and paid virtually no attention to the counselor; not surprisingly, their behavior did not sit well with her and prompted a quick deterioration of her talk into a severe scolding of the students. It seemed that both students and counselor were caught in a no-win situation but of course the stakes for the students were, ultimately, far higher.

According to the students in room 134, the guidance counselors (both at their middle schools and at Prairie Heights) have a great deal of power when those all-important decisions about classes are being made. Without exception, these students came from families that placed a high value on education; most of the parents understood their role as first-generation immigrants and had high hopes that their children would be better off financially and would live more comfortably. Most of these parents also had scant direct interaction with the school, and were rarely the ones to initiate calls to or communication with a particular teacher or staff member. As previously discussed, many of them face several obstacles that make it hard to have quick access to their child's school. The parents work long hours in jobs that do not look kindly upon them taking off time in the middle of the day to run over to school, something middle class parents are often able to do with more ease.

A multicultural, multiracial group of kids that meets regularly at Prairie Heights spent one morning talking about the differences in counseling. The kids of color noted that they are routinely, almost programmatically, steered away from college prep courses, and pushed to go the technical school/community college route. One white girl ended up being sort of a 'control group' as she had the same advisor, and was set on doing an associate degree in culinary arts at the local technical school. The advisor was very adamant that she 'had' to apply to a four-year college, and did not back off until the girl's mother intervened. Interestingly, this student was an immigrant, but from Eastern Europe.

After that conversation, I asked a small group of students in room 134 how many of them had taken their pre-college tests. Only Adela seemed to understand the sorting role played by these tests. Lalo dismissed the tests and, indeed, the whole idea of going on to school -- at least in the United States. He announced that he would be heading off to the UNAM (Mexico's prestigious National University). "It's the Harvard of Mexico," he added, which caused the other boys to erupt into laughter. I noted that he had a point, and we talked a little about the university's long history in Mexican life. Javier was more than a little angry. "Why?" he asked, "Why don't we *know* that?" They also talked about going into the trades, with both plumbing and auto mechanics mentioned as trades that someone they knew back in Mexico had practiced. Alex wanted to be an auto mechanic, like his uncle (who had settled in a small town near Lakeview) and seemed to be heading towards an unofficial apprenticeship with him. In any case, they were feeling their way forward on their own, with scant official help from Prairie Heights.

If some staff were seen as blocking (intentionally or not) student success, several teachers, including White teachers, were singled out by the students as being key to their success and/or happiness at school. Students praised those teachers who gave them a chance, got to know them and made them work hard. Several of the teachers had made connections with students by recruiting them for extracurricular activities and thus increasing the strength of the student-school connection. Javier noted that even those teachers who were potentially allies for him and his peers had their hands tied. "They know the problem, they see it, they see that it's bad, but they don't do anything, they can't do anything, …as much as they want to, well in a classroom, yes, I think they can do this in a classroom, everyone's equal, but not in the school."[135]

I asked all the students if there was one adult at the school who made a difference to them. Natalia told me about Ms. P. During her sophomore year, Ms. P was Natalia's teacher for her study skills class; she liked Ms. P but did not have too much ongoing contact with her until Ms. P. approached Natalia to join a club girls' sports team. She was very no-nonsense about outfitting Natalia with the proper equipment and uniforms, realizing that buying basic equipment might be an obstacle; but doing it in a way that felt okay to Natalia. That team became one of her lifelines to the school and she had a very successful career at school. She was quite adamant about pointing out to me that her two brothers were very smart and could have done very well at school, if someone like Ms. P had looked out for them.

Although there are a number of teachers like Ms. P, the very *structure* of the district and the school, alongside the embedded attitudes of much of the school staff (who often stand in opposition, if somewhat covert, to stated school and/or district policy) inform many of the decisions made at every level of the school. Thus many Latino students end up being routinely shut out of the possibilities of real success in high school. Structural decisions all too often end up in the hands of a few people who have serious amounts of power as well as the ability to greatly impact the lives of the Latino students.

Parents who are well-educated themselves (and generally, though not always, fairly comfortable in socioeconomic terms) function as gatekeepers or what more usefully be understood as *de facto* 'door openers' for their children. They understand what opportunities are available to their children, both within the school as well as in the larger community. They can often pay substantial amounts of money for 'extras' such as tutoring, music classes, sports equipment, etc. They know how to complete college applications and have a distinct advantage over many other families. While it is not only the Latino immigrant families who are at a disadvantage, they are in a particularly

---

[135]"Ellos saben el problema, ellos lo ven, saben que está mal, pero no hacen nada, no pueden hacer nada ... que por mucho que quieren ... bueno, en un salón, si, pienso que en un salón se puede hacer eso, están todos igual, pero en el colegio, no."

vulnerable position. In addition to issues of educational and financial resources, they must also deal with language barriers and the burden of undocumented immigration status that makes many families fearful of seeking extra help. For students from fairly comfortable economic backgrounds, several things are clear; their families have assumed from a fairly early age that they will do well and go on to college. Additionally, and perhaps more importantly, these parents are willing to intervene if they think that the school is not making the right decisions for their child. They are not only willing to intervene, but believe that it is their right to do so, and the school generally listens to them. Most of the parents of the Latino students had tenuous relations with the schools at best and were in no position to effectively advocate for their students. This should not necessarily be an issue, but some of the decisions made by guidance counselors demonstrate that there continues to be a problem. We see that social class is fundamentally linked to student success at Prairie Heights, but because class and race are often collapsed into one category, race actually continues to hold sway as the strongest sorting factor.

LANGUAGE AND OPPORTUNITY

Though many native Spanish speakers who enter the Lakeview system in the early primary grades now receive at least some instruction in Spanish, none of the students in room 134 had that experience. In many ways, they were on the margins of school life because they were not as fluent in English and ended up being tracked because of their 'lack of English,' rather than being seen as gifted given that they are in effect negotiating two languages and two cultures every single day.

A number of the native Spanish speakers at Prairie Heights, and this was certainly true for the majority of my interviewees, use Spanish on a daily basis with their close friends and almost exclusively with their families. However, a number of the 134 students have a very hard time with the grammar involved in writing Spanish, as most of them have been largely schooled in English-speaking contexts where Spanish was looked at as an obstacle to their learning English, rather than as a resource to cultivate and protect, even as they were learning English.

My study took place within the context of a Spanish language class for native Spanish speakers. Ms. Lawrence, the teacher in room 134, is a Spanish language teacher in the Lakeview district with more than 15 years of experience. As more native speakers began to show up in the halls of Prairie Heights, she remembers that her classes were oftentimes home to a few native speakers as well. She noted that the native speakers were often put on the spot in her traditional Spanish classes with questions such as, "How do *you* not know the accents?" often asked in incredulous tones. Students who had come to the US as young children were perfectly fluent in spoken Spanish but had few skills reading and writing their native language. Oscar mentioned his experience in a traditional Spanish class. "It was like I wasn't supposed to make even one mistake. Well, some of them probably aren't perfect in English class. It was weird, and also boring. I don't need to learn how to speak, but then all those kids who could only say, 'oh, ¿como estás?' were getting As." Classes that emphasize a less communicative style of language learning tend to privilege non-native speakers. Javier summed it up this way. "Well, I can read a book and talk about anything in it … but they get almost perfect grades, even though they can barely speak, just because they're filling out a ton of worksheets."[136] While many of the non-native speakers are clearly working hard and many do try to speak Spanish[137], the native speakers are rarely recognized, much less honored or respected for the expertise they already have, and few make it to the higher levels of Spanish where fluid communication would give them a definite edge.

This situation prompted Ms. Lawrence, one of the long-term Spanish teachers at Prairie Heights, to spearhead a class for Prairie Heights' native Spanish speakers to try and rectify some of the underlying inequalities in Spanish instruction at the school. Although a non-native Spanish speaker herself, Ms. Lawrence believes strongly in supporting native Spanish speakers towards academic mastery of their native language. Her Spanish for Spanish speakers class in room 134 became something of a home base for those students.

---

[136] "Bueno, yo puedo leer un libro y hablar de todo …pero ellos sacan notas casi perfectas, aunque casi ni pueden hablar, solo porque pueden llenar un montón de worksheets."

[137] Ironically, this often includes pricey language study programs in Spanish-speaking countries during the summer.

For the students in room 134, Spanish was a touchstone for home, for a place they had left behind. At least one scholar has referred to the concept of "cultural mourning" when talking about immigrant children and education (Ainslie, 1998) and that certainly resonated with my observations. Cultural mourning was most clearly articulated when students talked about their younger siblings (usually between 3-8 years difference in age), understanding those siblings as having 'lost' much of the culture for which they continued to yearn; certainly language was key and one of the most palpable signifiers, but it was not the only factor. Mexico continued to be an important point of reference, and they saw their younger siblings as losing that, without having gained much in the tradeoff.

With the resonance that language carries with it, it is not particularly surprising that a key reason for my relatively easy entrance into the classroom had to do with the fact that I speak Spanish, and not the Spanish students have come to expect from non-native speaking adults. After years of living in Central America, my Spanish was more similar to theirs than to the more formal Spanish used in the classroom. As I observed and spoke with the students during my two years of research, language policy and the language identity of the students was often front and center. Spanish was an important marker for the students, something they claimed and something that often served as a means of identifying their similarity to or underscoring their difference from, their peers. Language thus was a decisive element in determining the degree to which they were able to fully enter and, indeed, belong to the larger school community. The students both policed their own use of language (Spanish) even as they were subjected to the varying school-based language policies that have enormously impacted their school lives.

Valenzuela (1997) speaks quite eloquently about the problem of a model of so-called subtractive bilingualism, noting that far too many students who come to the US as native Spanish speakers not only lose their formal grounding in the Spanish language, they never gain the needed foundation in academic English. Thus, they are essentially caught in the middle as they do not end up mastering English, but neither do they maintain a strong foundation in Spanish. This premise mirrors what I saw with the students in room 134; their difficulties with Spanish grammar and formal language usage did not necessarily mean that they were able to easily negotiate formal English. Ms. Lawrence sometimes asked me to work with her students as they worked on written essays in Spanish. Working with Luis one day on reviewing a short essay, I saw how frustrated he was. He complained about all the '*pinche*' accents and grammatical hoops though which he had to jump. "¿Por qué importa?!?!" he whined. "Ud. me entiende." ["Why does it matter? You understand me."] Ms. Lawrence tried to be very up front about what she saw as the considerable disadvantage they faced, and worked at convincing them that they needed to be unassailable in terms of their academic Spanish. This argument was fairly persuasive to some of the students. As students spoke and (rarely) wrote in English in Ms. Lawrence's classroom, their incomplete knowledge of academic English was obvious, yet there didn't seem to be a school-based response to this issue. Ms. Lawrence mentioned a number of times that she was worried about their English, noting that it would hurt not only their chances for further study but seriously restrict their job options as well. Ultimately the struggle is about power, as the belief that Spanish as a language is less important than English, and thus not worthy of maintaining, continues to hold sway precisely because the immigrant students who speak Spanish are seen as less important, and in some ways, less academically successful or sophisticated than their English speaking peers.

At the same time, it was quite noteworthy that some of the students, in terms of verbal language, were highly skilled at moving back and forth between English, and, of course, of using and co-creating a form of Spanglish specific to their particularities as immigrant students in the Lakeview community. That Spanglish was favored, as it offered them a way to communicate with each other and marked them as unique, and strengthened the bonds they already had. Many of them referred to well-known locations such as parks and grocery stores with a Spanglish-ized (Adela's term) moniker. The two sides of town became El East and El West. Certain Spanglish terms common along the border, for example "*troca*" rather than *camión* for truck, are used daily among the students, and at the same time, many English words (for example, as mentioned earlier, "worksheet") associated with school have slipped into usage when they are speaking Spanish. Using mildly offensive words as terms of endearment or fondness (among both boys and girls) was also common and another way for the students to reclaim territory long seen as second class.

While Spanglish had infiltrated their Spanish to a certain degree, the students understood the weight and status of formal, academic Spanish. There was constant bickering when one student thought another student wasn't speaking 'real' Spanish – they made fun of each other if they were not seen to be quick enough with their Spanish slang, etc. This was also used as a way to claim identity; for example, David, US-born and proudly identified as Chicano, took a great deal of (not all good-natured) teasing from the other students about the fact that he made so many errors in both his written and his spoken Spanish. "Son malos,"[138] he said to them on more than one occasion, not entirely in jest; justifying the fact that he had lost some of his Spanish by his mother's decision to emphasize his English. David explained that they lived in what he described as a "jerky redneck town" during most of his elementary school years, and so he defended his mother's decision as the right one at the time. While David's mother did speak both English and Spanish quite well, the social circumstances of where they lived during David's childhood obliged her to raise him almost exclusively in English. He heard and spoke enough Spanish to be a good fit for Ms. Lawrence's class, but he did put up with a lot from his classmates. Somewhat ironically, perhaps, he also saw the class as a haven of sorts; "I don't speak Spanish that great," he admitted one day, "but I am Latino and this class is just kinda cool that way." A Spanish-speaking student who was not in Ms. Lawrence's class told me that he had initially felt he didn't really 'fit in' with the other Latino students, until they realized that he spoke Spanish, and quite well. Both of his parents were professionals, and citizens, and so some of the issues that exacted daily pressure on the students in room 134 simply did not affect him.

Even as Spanish-speaking students seemed to have their native language used against them, they seemed to intuitively understand that speaking Spanish represented an important choice, at once psychic and political, and one through which they could assert a strong sense of identity. Spanish defined membership in a particular world, even as it meant they would likely never gain full access to the "real" world at Prairie Heights. Ironically, their Spanish was not considered to be 'proper' Spanish by many of the other Spanish teachers and left many

---

[138] "You guys are bad".

of the students in somewhat undefined territory, with neither the recognition their language reality deserved, nor the full assistance they needed to effectively master English.

Opportunities abound at Prairie Heights for those who are connected or 'hooked in' to how the school functions, as well as to the key people who can ease transitions and facilitate success. While all students must deal with the internal structures of gatekeepers as they seek opportunities, Latino students did have to deal with several additional difficulties. Most of the students in room 134 had parents who worked long hours (often at two or more jobs), did not have high levels of formal education and struggled with English. All of that made it difficult for them to have the kind of access to school that the middle-class, educated parents (not all White, but overwhelmingly so) generally took for granted. For the students of room 134, the structuring of opportunity, whether around language issues or course assignments and post-secondary plans, and in spite of many individual teachers' attempts to individually override the system, was simply out of their hands and thus, beyond their reach.

Chapter 6

A Changing Landscape

I began this study with the aim of identifying some of the factors underlying the poor achievement rates of Latino students at Prairie Heights High School, initially focusing on understanding how issues of cultural, racial and linguistic identity play out in their daily school lives. I walked through the door of Prairie Heights at the outset of my study with a fairly clear sense of the context in which the students of room 134 were experiencing school. However, my ongoing contact with those students fine-tuned my understanding, and gave me a far more nuanced sense of what the students face and where they are going. My time in room 134 deeply affected my sense of how complex each student's life is, and how much is at stake for each of them in terms of their educational potential and success. The experiences of the students in room 134 weave together the shifting realities of race, language and legal status in the context of a school's institutional stance. The experiences of the students in room 134 inform a broader understanding of Latino students and offer a small, but essential, slice of a larger reality. My findings were several, offering insight into the experiences of Latino students at a school site undergoing unprecedented demographic changes and pointing to directions for future research.

REDRAWING THE RACIAL MAP

I will first consider the issue of race and what I found at Prairie Heights. The school has an extremely complicated history around the issue of race and achievement, dating back a number of decades. Until recently, that racial context was almost exclusively black and white.

However, the racial terrain at Prairie Heights has undergone fairly thorough-going shifts in recent years (and the trend seems to be continuing) that has led to what I understand as a remapping of the school's racial hierarchy. My time in room 134 and my sense as well of what is happening in the larger Lakeview community underscored the ongoing weight of race as one of the key sorting factors in students' lives, with the attendant impact on academic status and success. While Prairie Heights has a diverse student body, and a dynamic that many experience as generally welcoming and friendly, the racial stratification remains. There is ongoing discussion about the 'achievement gap' (referred to by some as the 'opportunity gap') but little of substance has been done to change the larger context in which many policy decisions are made.

What I saw and heard from the students in room 134 showed me several things. They had, consciously or not, both intuited and absorbed the Black/White binary that in many ways still governs many of the decisions that the Lakeview district makes about its schools and one that continues to have an impact on Prairie Heights. Many of the students experienced race as something used to define them or shape expectations of them on the part of school staff. The students understand themselves as located beyond the real focal point of power in the school, and have scant hope of obtaining full status. Though this is linked to their legal status, that is not the only reason. They understand themselves as culturally and racially different than most of their peers, and are both proud of that as well as cognizant of the challenges they face as a result. After two years in room 134, I would also argue that, though the racial map in Lakeview schools is shifting dramatically—the two most dramatic changes being increasing numbers of Latino students and a steady decline in White students--in many ways it is also quite rigid. The white norm at the school remains unchallenged, and is consistently held up as a model which other students should (or should want to) aspire to. Latino students are near the bottom of the heap, but that bottom is constantly shifting, while the top is fairly static and largely impervious to change. I witnessed a situation in which the students of color continue to jockey for status as the more 'favored minority' – even in a context where they have become the numerical majority. I use the concept 'favored minority' as it seems to be the lens used by those making the decisions at the level of the district and school, and who seem unwilling to effect a serious or authentic shake-up in racial distinctions. It does seem to be the case that the Latino students, in part because of raced notions of whiteness, are accorded a bit more status and understanding than their African American peers at Prairie Heights.

THE BORDER AND BELONGING

It was clear from my first days in room 134 that immigration, like race and the racialization of school space, was something that would figure into my analysis of the students in that classroom. I had not fully absorbed, however, the nearly incalculable impact and presence of the border, despite the enormous physical distance between the actual US-Mexican border and Prairie Heights High School. While it was palpable to the students in terms of what it represented as a break with their cultural, linguistic and geographic roots, it also had a force in their lives that played out on a less defined, psychic, level. At the same time, for the students in room 134 (and in many classrooms across the Lakeview district, for that matter) the most profound impact of the border is felt in the weight of their legal status. Though I never ascertained the precise number (of course, no official data is kept), the overwhelming majority of the students in room 134 over the course of the two years I spent there did not have legal papers. This meant many things, from not being able to legally obtain a job to living in fear of run-ins with law enforcement that could lead to the involvement of ICE agents to the reality that leaving the US to be part of extended family events in Mexico meant risking the possibility of not being able to get 'back in'. In short, it means that the border is defining factor in their lives. Whether or not a high school student has papers, of course, does not affect his or her presence at school. School officials are not supposed to ask about immigration status and by all accounts, both the Lakeview district as a whole and Prairie Heights have been very good about adhering to this. The border, though, profoundly affects students' own sense of their potential and what their future might be. And, of course, once they are past the secondary stage, the doors begin to close with great force, if not open violence. Students can technically apply to any school, but the all-important FAFSA (the federal government's financial aid form) requires a social security number. These daily concerns continue to play out as a political firestorm around the issue of immigration gathers force, sacrificing students' educational futures and sense of security in their daily lives to a highly politicized struggle that scarcely took into account real people or the impact of legislation on their lives. The recent DACA (Deferred Action for Childhood Arrivals) legislation, signed into law by President Obama in June, 2012) bought many students a two-year respite, but their long-term status remains up in the air.

GATEKEEPERS AND THE STRUCTURING OF OPPORTUNITY

Looking at a Prairie Heights course catalog, or paging through the school's monthly bulletin, one is struck by the variety of courses available as well as the range of extra-curricular activities. Opportunities abound at the school, and are often referenced in public statements about Prairie Heights and its students. Yet those opportunities are not accessible to all. A relatively small number of what I call "gatekeepers" play key roles at Prairie Heights in their ability to either open or close doors to students. Though all students are affected by these gatekeepers, there is a disproportionate impact on Latino students for several reasons.[139] Many parents of the students in room 134 had difficulties negotiating school (as well as other public spaces) in English, and so were quite far removed 'from the loop', so to speak. Additionally, most of the parents did not have any direct experience with higher education in their home countries, much less in the US. Thus the maze of negotiating that key transition to post-secondary success poses nearly insurmountable problems for most of these parents. As the number of parents who represent the white 'norm' in the Lakeview school district (mostly white, highly educated, middle or upper middle class and able to skillfully manage key school transition points for their children) declines, the district shows some signs of focusing more on those parents. While the intention may not be (and likely is not) to ignore other students, that is often the result, as staff time is limited to begin with, and increasingly so as budget cuts continue. At the same time, the 134 students did point to particular staff members who were key to their sense of belonging at Prairie

---

[139]The impact on African-American students has been devastating and has been written about at the national level. Certainly more attention to this would be welcome in the context of Prairie Heights or similar schools.

Heights as well as central to connecting them with other opportunities—both academic and extracurricular. While those individual staff members played important roles, in the end the institutional structures carried more weight. Had different individuals occupied some of the key positions at the school (assistant principals, guidance counselors, etc.), the outcome may well have been different for the students in room 134.

WHAT LIES AHEAD

The Lakeview schools have been working diligently, if not always uniformly, to adapt language instruction in order to respond more effectively to the growing Latino population. While many elementary schools have transitioned from traditional ESL programs to bilingual instruction at the grade school level, some of the Lakeview elementary schools are now offering dual language instruction. This raises several questions. We will want to carefully follow the students, both the native Spanish speakers and the native English speakers, and see what the medium and long-term results are in terms of literacy and academic preparedness. At the same time, some anecdotal evidence from those programs points to their potential as wedges that could widen the gap between black and white students, with the Latino students somehow 'hopscotching' over their peers of color. Might this be an instance of interest convergence, as the district struggles to hold on to its White parents, particularly at the elementary school level? Or will the considerable educational and cultural resources and wealth that the Latino students bring to the district and to Lakeview as a whole be honored in such a way that they can flourish, and help to recast the schools and community in a way that more accurately reflects the demographic changes and cultural possibilities at hand? The students of room 134 have long since left that classroom, and Prairie Heights, behind. They, and their peers who have followed them at Prairie Heights, are caught in a moment of an often nasty backlash against immigrants and the hot and cold attitude of the larger Lakeview community that does not quite know where it stands. The students are, in many ways, pawns in a political battle they did not create and whose consequences they do not deserve. I salute their resilience and hope for changes in the political winds.

Where Are They Now?

Though some time has passed since I left Room 134, I have been able to keep up a bit with what the students are doing now. There are several students I see every now and then, and they have filled me in on what some of the others are doing.

*Adela is enrolled in a small private college in Lakeview. She won a full tuition scholarship, lives at home and is working to help with the rent. She is doing well, though reports that she has had to take several remedial courses in order to catch up. She hopes to be a psychologist or a social worker. Her mother reported crying and jumping up and down when she heard the news about the scholarship, and said it had long been "her dream" for Adela to go to college. She applied for and received DACA status.

*Natalia also went to a private college, at some distance from Lakeview.

* Maria is attending a community college and has gotten involved in a number of community groups, particularly arts-based organizations. She busses tables, and occasionally hosts, at a local restaurant

* Despite initial plans to attend the local university, Camila joined the army and has visited Ms. Lawrence's class several times, though Ms. Lawrence worries that she glamorizes military life. She is currently deployed in Afghanistan.

*Carmen dropped out of Prairie Heights, ran afoul of the law and is currently awaiting sentencing as an accomplice to murder.

* Emilio cannot be located. Rumors are that he was deported, though that could not be confirmed.

*Ricardo has worked a series of jobs at local restaurants. He hopes to go to the local community college today, but is currently finishing up his GED, as he did not earn enough credits for a high school diploma. He applied for and received DACA status.

* Victor, originally set on becoming a cop, ended up becoming a father one week before he graduated from high school. Both he and his girlfriend (now wife, as they married right before the baby was born) enrolled at the local community college, but ended up dropping out for financial reasons.

* David barely graduated from high school and ran into trouble with some petty drug use. He was put on probation and is currently studying at the local community college, with the dream of becoming a commercial artist.

* Javier also became a father, and is going to the local community college half-time. He continues to be a well-known player in Lakeview's Latino soccer leagues.

* Oscar attends the same college as Adela. His girlfriend is attending the local community college for an associate degree. They plan to get married once he finishes and then have children. He says, "I really didn't want to do that (have a kid so soon) to my parents…" He applied for and received DACA status.

* Luis left Prairie Heights for an apprenticeship program, where he was able to earn his GED at the same time.

* Alex has been in and out of court, on charges ranging from underage drinking to disorderly conduct. He is facing possible deportation.

* Cerina got pregnant, dropped out of Prairie Heights and moved in with her boyfriend's family.

* Domingo is attending the local community college, and hoping to transfer to a larger university soon, those his grades may make that difficult.

References

Abi-Nader, J. (1987). *'A House for My Mother': An Ethnography of Motivational Strategies in a Successful College Preparatory Program for Hispanic High School Students.* Dissertation . Georgia State University.

Acuña, R. (1981). *Occupied America: A History of the Chicano.* New York: Harper & Row.

- (1998). Greasers Go Home: Mexican Immigration, the 1920s. In Delgado, Richard and Jean Stefancic, eds. *The Latino/a Condition: A Critical Reader.* New York: New York University Press.

Ainslie, R.C. (1998). Cultural mourning, immigration, and engagement: Vignettes from the Mexican experience. In M.M. Suárez-Orozco (Ed.) *Crossings: Mexican immigration in interdisciplinary perspective..* Cambridge: Harvard University Press.

Anzaldúa, G. (1987). *Borderlands/La Frontera: The New Mestiza.* San Francisco: Aunt Lute.

Apple, M.W. (1990). 2nd edition. *Ideology and Curriculum.* New York: Routledge.

-(1993). *Official Knowledge: Democratic Education in a Conservative Age.* New York: Routledge.

- (2001). *Educating the "Right" Way: Markets, Standards, God and Inequality.* New York: Routledge.

Appleby, C., Moreno, N. and A. Smith. (2009). Setting Down Roots: Tlacotepense Settlement in the United States. In W.A. Cornelius, D. Fitzgerald, J. Hernández-Díaz and S. Borger. Eds. *Migration from the Mexican Mixteca.* Eds., San Diego: Center for Comparative Immigration Studies at the University of California.

Arriola, E. (1997). LatCrit Theory, International Human Rights, Popular Culture, and the Faces of Despair in INS Raids. *Inter-American Law Review 28 (2):* 245-262.

Au, K.H. (1993). *Literacy Instruction in Multicultural Settings.* Ft. Worth, TX: Harcourt Brace College Publishers.

Balderrama, F. and R. Rodriguez. (2006). *Decade of Betrayal: Mexican Repatriation in the 1930s.* Albuquerque: University of New Mexico Press.

Ballenger, C. (1999). *Teaching Other People's Children: Literacy and Learning in a Bilingual Classroom.* New York: Teachers College Press.

Barajas, H.L. and A. Ronnkvist. (2007). Racialized Space: Framing Latino and Latina Experience in Public Schools. *Teachers College Press, 109:6,* 1517-1538.

Bell, D. (1980). Brown v. Board of Education and the interest-convergence dilemma. *Harvard Law Review, 93,* 518.
   - (1987). *And we will not be saved: The elusive quest for racial justice.* New York: Basic Books.
   - (1995). Brown v. Board of Education and the Interest Convergence Dilemma. In Crenshaw, K., N. Gotanda, G. Peller and K. Thomas. (Eds.) *Critical Race Theory: The Key Writings That Formed the Movement.* New York: The New Press.

Beverly, J. (1989). "The Margin at the Center: On *Testimonio* (Testimonial Narrative)". *Modern Fiction Studies,* 33 (1), 11-28.
   -(1993). El testimonio en la encrucijada. *Revista Iberoamericana 164-165:* 485-495.
   - (2000). Testimonio, subalternity and narrative authority. In N.K. Denzin & Y.S. Lincoln (Eds.), *Handbook of qualitative research* (2nd ed., 555-565). Thousand Oaks, CA: Sage.
   -(2004). *Testimonio: on the politics of truth.* Minneapolis: The University of Minnesota Press.

Blau, J.R. (2003). *Race in the schools: Perpetuating white dominance?* Boulder, CO: Lynne Rienner Publishers.

Bonilla-Silva, E. (2006). *Racism without Racists: Color-Blind Racism and the Persistence of Racial Inequality in the United States.* Lanham, Maryland: Rowman & Littlefield Publishers, Inc.

Carrasco, G.P. (1998). Latinos in the United States: Invitation and Exile. In R. Delgado and J. Stefancic. Eds. *The Latino Condition: A Critical Reader.* New York: New York University Press.

Carter, T.P. (1970). *Mexican Americans in School: A History of Educational Neglect*. Princeton: College Entrance Examination Board.

Casanova, U. (2010). *Si Se Puede!: Learning from a High School That Beats the Odds*. New York: Teachers College Press.

Cho, M.K. and M.W. Apple. (1998). Schooling, Work and Subjectivity. *British Journal of Sociology of Education, Vol. 19, No. 3.*

Collier, V. (1995). *Promoting Academic Success for ESL Students.* Jersey City: New Jersey Teachers of English to Speakers of Other Languages-Bilingual Educators.

Crawford, J. (1989). *Bilingual Education: History, Politics, Theory and Practice*. Trenton, N.J.: Crane.

Crenshaw, K. (1995). Mapping the Margins: Intersectionality, Identity Politics, and Violence Against Women of Color. In Crenshaw, K., Gotanda, N., Peller, G., and Thomas, K. (Eds.) *Critical Race Theory: The Key Writings That Formed the Movement*. New York: The New Press.

Crenshaw, K, Gotanda, N., Peller, G. and Thomas, K. (1995). *Critical Race Theory: The Key Writings that Formed the Movement.* New York: The New Press.

Crowley, M., D. Lichter and Z. Qian. (2006). Beyond Gateway Cities: Economic Restructuring and Poverty Among Mexican Immigrant Families and Children. *Family Relations, 55,* 345–360.

Cummins, J. (1981). The role of primary language development in promoting educational success for language minority students. In *Schooling and Language Minority Students: A Theoretical Framework*. Sacramento, CA: Office of Bilingual Bicultural Education:
- (1989). *Empowering Minority Students.* Sacramento: California Association for Bilingual Education.
- (2000). *Language, Power and Pedagogy: Bilingual Children in the Crossfire*. Clevedon, UK: Multilingual Matters.

Darder, A. (1995). Buscando América: The Contributions of Critical Latino Educators to the Academic Development and Empowerment of Latino Students in the U.S. In C. Sleeter and P. McLaren. Eds. *Multicultural Education, Critical Pedagogy, and the Politics of Difference*. Albany: State University of New York Press.
- (1997). Creating the Conditions for Cultural Democracy in the

Classroom. In Darder, A., R.D. Torres and H. Gutiérrez. *Latinos and Education: A Critical Reader*. New York: Routledge.

Darder, A. and Torres, R. (2004). *After Race: Racism After Multiculturalism*. New York: New York University Press.

Darder, A., Torres, R.D., & Gutiérrez, H. (Eds). (1997). *Latinos and education: A critical reader*. Boston: Routledge.

Davila, E.R. and Aviles de Bradley, A. (2010). Examining Education for Latinas/os in Chicago: A CRT/LatCrit Approach. *Educational Foundations, Vol. 24, n.1-2*, 39-58.

DeGenova, N. and Ramos-Zayas, A. (2003). *Latino Crossings: Mexicans, Puerto Ricans and the Politics of Race and Citizenship*. New York: Routledge.

De León, A. (1983). *They Called Them Greasers: Anglo Attitudes Toward Mexicans in Texas, 1821-1900*. Austin: University of Texas Press.

Delgado, R. (1991). Affirmative Action as a Majoritarian Device: Or, Do You Really Want to Be a Role Model? *Michigan Law Review 89:* 1222.
-- (2000). Storytelling for Oppositionists and Others: A Plea for Narrative. In R. Delgado and J. Stefancic (Eds.). *Critical Race Theory: The Cutting Edge*, 2nd Edition. Philadelphia: Temple University Press.\

Delgado, R. and Stefancic, J., Eds. (1998). *The Latino/a Condition: A Critical Reader*. New York: New York University Press.
-Eds.(2000). 2nd Edition. *Critical Race Theory: The Cutting Edge*. Philadelphia: Temple University Press.

Delgado Bernal, D. (2006). Rethinking Grassroots Activism: Chicana Resistance in the 1968 East Los Angeles School Blowouts. In M.W. Apple and K. Buras (Eds). *The Subaltern Speak: Curriculum, Power and Educational Struggles*. New York: Routledge.

Delgado-Gaitan, C. (1991). *Crossing Cultural Borders: Education for Immigrant Families in America*. NY: Falmer Press.

Delpit, L. (1995). *Other People's Children: Cultural Conflict in the Classroom*. New York: The New Press.

Díaz, E. and B. Flores. (2001). Teacher as Sociocultural, Sociohistorical Mediator: Teaching to the Potential. In Reyes, María de la Luz and Halcón, John J., eds. *The Best for Our*

Children: Critical Perspectives on Literacy for Latino Students.
New York: Teachers College Press.

Díaz Soto, L. (1997). *Language, Culture, and Power: Bilingual Families and the Struggle for Quality Education.* Albany: State University of New York Press.

Dixson, A.D. and C.K. Rousseau. Eds. (2006). *Critical Race Theory in Education: All God's Children Got a Song.* New York: Routledge.

Doane. A,W., & Bonilla-Silva, E. (2003). *White out.* New York: Routledge.

Donato, R. (1997). *The Other Struggle for Equal Schools: Mexican Americans during the Civil Rights Era.* Albany: State University of New York Press.

Duarte-Herrera, C.A. (2001). Defining the US-Mexico Border as Hyperreality. *Estudios Fronterizos, vol. 2, no. 4.*

DuBois, W.E.B. (1903). *The Souls of Black Folk.* New York: Fine Creative Media.

Durand, J. and D. Massey. (2004). *Crossing the border: research from the Mexican Migration Project.* New York: Russell Sage Foundation.

Escárcega, S. and S. Varese. (2004). *La ruta mixteca: el impacto etnopolítico de la migración trasnacional en los pueblos indígenas de México.* Dirección General de Publicaciones y Fomento Editorial, Universidad Nacional Autónoma de Mexico.

Feagin, J.R. (2001). *Racist America: Roots, current realities, & future reparations.* New York: Routledge.

Feagin, J.R. and M.P. Sikes. (1994). *Living with Racism: The Black Middle-Class Experience.* Boston: Beacon Press.

Félix, A., González, C. and Ramírez, R. (2008). Political Protest, Ethnic Media and Latino Naturalization. *American Behavioral Scientist 52*:618.

Fernández, L. (2002). Telling stories about school: Using Critical Race and Latino Critical Theories to document Latina/Latino Education and Resistance. *Qualitative Inquiry, 8 (1)*, 45-65.

Fine, M., Weis, L., Powell, L. and Wong, L. Eds. (1997). *Off White: Readings on Race, Power and Society.* New York: Routledge.

Flores, L. (2003). Constructing Rhetorical Borders: Peons, Illegal Aliens and Competing Narratives of Immigration. *Critical Studies in Media Communication. Vol. 20, no. 4*, 362-387.

Gans, H. (1979). Symbolic ethnicity: The future of ethnic groups and cultures in America. *Ethnic and Racial Studies, 2,* 1-18.

- (2009). The Possibility of a New Racial Hierarchy in the Twenty-First Century United States. In C.A. Gallagher, Ed. *Rethinking the Color Line: Readings in Race and Ethnicity.* 4th Ed. New York: McGraw-Hill.

García, E. (2001). *Hispanic Education in the United States.* Lanham, MD: Rowman & Littlefield Publishers.

Garcia, R. (1995). Critical Race Theory and Proposition 187: The Racial Politics of Immigration Law. *Chicano-Latino Law Review. Fall 1995*: 17.

Gillborn, D. (2009). Education Policy as an Act of White Supremacy: Whiteness, Critical Race Theory, and Education Reform. In Taylor, E., D. Gillborn and G. Ladson-Billings, *Foundations of Critical Race Theory in Education.* New York: Routledge, 2009.

Gonzalez, G.G. (1990). *Chicano Education in the Era of Segregation.* Philadelphia: Balch Institute Press.

Gonzalez, J. (2000). *Harvest of Empire: A History of Latinos in America.* New York: Penguin.

Goodwin, A. Lin. (2002). Teacher Preparation and the Education of Immigrant Children. *Education and Urban Society, Vol. 32, No. 2.*

Gotanda, N. (2003). Reflections on Korematsu, Brown and white innocence. *Temple Political & Civil Rights Law Review. Vol. 13*: 663.

Guérin-Gonzalez, C. (1994). *Mexican Workers and American Dreams: Immigration, Repatriation, and California Farm Labor, 1900-1939.* New Brunswick, N.J.: Rutgers University Press.

Gutiérrez, D.G. (1996). Sin Fronteras? Chicanos, Mexican Americans and the Emergence of the Contemporary Mexican Immigration Debate. In Gutiérrez, David, ed. *Between Two Worlds: Mexican Immigrants in the United States.* Wilmington, DE: Scholarly Resources.

Gutiérrez, K. (2005/2006). White Innocence: A Framework and Methodology for Rethinking Educational Discourse and Inquiry. UCLA, United States of America *International Journal of Learning.* www.Learning-Journal. Gutiérrez, K., Asato, J., Santos, M., and Gotanda, N. (2002). Backlash pedagogy: Language and culture and the politics of reform. *The Review of Education, Pedagogy, and Cultural Studies, 24 (4),* 335-351.

Gutiérrez, K., Asato, J., Pacheco, M., Moll, L., Olson, K., Horng, E.L., Ruiz, R., Garcia, E. and McCarty T. (2002). "Sounding American": The consequences of new reforms on English language learners. *Reading Research Quarterly, 37 (3)* 328-343.

Gutiérrez, R. (1995). Historical and Social Science Research on Mexican Americans. In J.A. Banks, Ed., *Handbook of Research on Multicultural Education.* New York: Simon and Schuster Macmillan.

Hacker, A. (1992). *Two Nations: Black and White, Separate, Hostile, Unequal.* New York: Scribner.

Hall, S. (1987). Gramsci and Us. *Marxism Today. June 1987*: 16-21.

Haney López, I.F. (2000). Race and Erasure: The Salience of Race to Latinos/as. In R. Delgado and J. Stefancic (Eds.) *Critical Race Theory: The Cutting Edge.* 2nd Edition. Philadelphia: Temple University Press.
(2006). *White by Law: The Legal Construction of Race.* New York: New York University Press.

Hayduk, R. (2009). Radical responses to neoliberalism: Immigrant rights in the global era. *Dialectical Anthropology 33:2.*

Hernández-Sheets, R. (1995). From Remedial to Gifted: Effects of Culturally Centered Pedagogy. *Theory into Practice 34:34.*

Hernández-Truyol, B.E. (1998). Building Bridge: Latinas and Latinos at the Crossroads. In Delgado, Richard and Jean Stefancic, eds. *The Latino/a Condition: A Critical Reader.* New York: New York University Press.

Hirsch-Dubin, F. (2006). Evolution of a Dream: The Emergence of Mayan Ethnomathematics and Indigenous ways of Knowing at a Mayan Autonomous School in Chiapas, Mexico. Paper presented at International Ethnomathematics Conference, Auckland, New Zealand.

Howard, T.C. (2008). "Who really cares?" The disenfranchisement of African American males in PreK-12 schools: A critical race theory perspective. *Teachers College Record, 110(5)*, 954-985.
- (2010). *Why Race and Culture Matter in Schools: Closing the Achievement Gap in America's Classrooms.* New York: Teachers College Press.

Huber, L.P., Huidor, O., Malagon, M., Sanchez, G., and Solórzano, D. (2006). Falling through the cracks: Critical transitions in the Latino/a educational pipeline. Los Angeles: UCLA Chicano

Studies Research Center. Ignatiev, Noel. (1996). *How the Irish Became White*. New York: Routledge.

Irizarry, J.G. (2005). Representin' for Latino students: Culturally responsive pedagogies, teacher identities, and the preparation of teachers for urban schools. Dissertation. University of Massachusetts-Amherst.

Jesse, D., Davis, A., and N. Pokorny. (2004). High-Achieving Middle Schools for Latino Students in Poverty. *Journal of Education for Students Placed at Risk (JESPAR), 9:1*, 23-45.

Kailin, J. (1996). *Engaging Teachers in Anti-Racist Pedagogy: An Historical and Ethnographic Study*. University of Wisconsin-Madison.

Kier, J. (2007*). "We asked for workers and they sent us people": A critical race theory and Latino critical theory ethnography exploring college-ready undocumented high school immigrants in North Carolina*. Dissertation. The University of North Carolina at Chapel Hill.

Kozol, J. (1991). *Savage Inequalities: Children in America's Schools*. New York: Crown.
- (2005). *The Shame of the Nation: The Restoration of Apartheid Schooling in America*. New York: Three Rivers Press.

Krashen, S. (1981). *Second Language Acquisition and Second Language Learning*. Oxford: Pergamon.
-(1996). *Under Attack: The Case Against Bilingual Education*. Culver City, CA: Language Education Associates.

Ladson-Billings, G. (1994). *The Dreamkeepers: Successful Teachers of African American Children*. San Francisco: Jossey-Bass Publishers.
-(1995). But That's Just Good Teaching! The Case for Culturally Relevant Pedagogy. *Theory into Practice. Vol. 34, no. 3.*
-(1995). Toward A Theory of Culturally Relevant Pedagogy. *American Educational Research Journal, Vol. 32, No.3.*
-(2000). Fighting for Our Lives: Preparing Teachers to Teach African American Students. *Journal of Teacher Education, 56*: 206-214.
- (2002). Avoiding a Second Harvest of Shame. Speech given at the Minority Achievement Network Conference, May, 2002.

Ladson-Billings, G. and W.F. Tate. (1994). Toward a theory of critical race theory in education. *Teachers College Record, 97*, 47-68.

- Eds. (2006). *Education Research in the Public Interest: Social Justice, Action, and Policy.* New York: Teachers College Press.

Lee, S. (2002). Learning "America": Hmong American High School Students. *Education and Urban Society. Vol 34, No. 2.*
- (2005). *Up Against Whiteness: Race, School and Immigrant Youth.* New York: Teachers College Press.

Lewis, A. E. (2003). *Race in the schoolyard: Negotiating the color line in classrooms and communities.* New Brunswick, N.J.: Rutgers University Press.

Limón, J.E. (1998). *American Encounters: Greater Mexico, The United States and the Erotics of Culture.* Boston: Beacon Press.

Lipsitz, G. (1998). *The possessive investment in whiteness: How white people profit from identity politics.* Philadelphia: Temple University Press.

López, G. (2001). The value of hard work: Lessons on parent involvement from an (im)migrant household. *Harvard Educational Review, 71 (3),* 416-437.

Lugo, A. (1997). "Reflections on border theory, culture, and the nation". In S. Michaelson and D.E. Johnson. Eds. *Border Theory: The Limits of Cultural Politics.* Minneapolis: University of Minnesota Press.
-(2005). Reflections on Border Theory, Culture and the Nation. In C. McCarthy, W. Crichlow, G. Dimitriadis and N. Dolby (Eds.). *Race, Identity and Representation.* 2nd Edition. New York: Taylor & Francis Group, LLC.
-(2008). *Fragmented Lives, Assembled Parts: Culture, Capitalism, and Conquest at the U.S.-Mexico Border.* Austin: University of Texas Press.

Mallon, F.E. (2001). Bearing Witness in Hard Times: Ethnography and Testimonio in a Postrevolutionary Age. In G.M. Joseph (Ed.) *Reclaiming the Political in Latin American History: Essays from the North.* Durham/London: Duke University Press.

Martínez, G. (2010). *Learning from Proposition 187: California's Past is Arizona's Prologue.* Washington, D.C.: The Center for American Progress.

Martínez, G.A. (2000). Mexican Americans and Whiteness. In, *Critical Race Theory : The Cutting Edge*, 2nd Edition, edited by Richard Delgado and Jean Stefancic. Philadelphia: Temple University Press, 2000.

Massey, D.S. (1997). What's driving Mexico-US migration? A
    theoretical, empirical, and policy analysis. *The American Journal
    of Sociology.*

Minami, M. and C.J. Ovando. (1995). Language Issues in
    Multicultural Contexts. In *Handbook of Research on Multicultural
    Education,* Banks, J.A.,Ed. New York: Simon and Schuster
    Macmillan.

Moll, L.C. (2001). The Diversity of Schooling: A Cultural and
    Historical Approach. In Reyes, María de la Luz and John J.
    Halcón, eds. *The Best for Our Children: Critical Perspectives on
    Literacy for Latino Students.* New York: Teachers College Press.

Moll, L.C., C. Amanti, D. Neff and N. González. (1992). "Funds of
    Knowledge for Teaching: Using a Qualitative Approach to
    Connect Homes and Classrooms". *Theory into Practice, Volume
    36, Number 2.*

Montejano, D. (1987). *Anglos and Mexicans in the Making of Texas.*
    Austin: University of Texas Press, 1987.

Moran, C.E. and K. Hakuta. (1995). Bilingual Education: Broadening
    Research Perspectives. In J.A. Banks (Ed). *Handbook of Research
    on Multicultural Education.* New York: Simon and Schuster
    Macmillan.

Morse, P.H. (1999). *Resilience as recovery from risk: An ecocultural
    framework for understanding Latino student school success.*
    Dissertation. University of California-Los Angeles.

Moses, R.P. and C. E. Cobb, Jr. (2001). *Radical Equations: Civil
    Rights from Mississippi to the Algebra Project.* Boston: Beacon
    Press.

Muñoz, C. (1989). *Youth, identity, power: the Chicano movement.*
    New York: Verso.

Navarro, A. (1998). *The Cristal Experiment: A Chicano Struggle for
    Community Control.* Madison: The University of Wisconsin Press.

Ngai, M.M. (2004). Impossible Subjects: Illegal Aliens and the
    Making of Modern America. Princeton: Princeton University
    Press.

Nieri, T.A. (2007). *School composition and the acculturation
    experience: How classmates shape Latino students' cultural
    identity.* Dissertation. Arizona State University.

Nieto, S. (1992). *Affirming Diversity: The Sociopolitical Context of
    Multicultural Education.* New York: Longman Press.

-(2002). *Language, Culture and Teaching: Critical Perspectives for a New Century.* Mahwah, NJ: Lawrence Erlbaum Associates.

Noguera, P.A. (2007). How Listening to Students Can Help Schools to Improve. *Theory Into Practice. 46 (3),* 205-211.

-(2008). *The Trouble with Black Boys ... and Other Reflections on Race, Equity, and the Future of Public Education.* San Francisco: Jossey-Bass.

Obidah, J.E. and K.M. Teel. (2001). *Because of the Kids: Facing Racial and Cultural Differences in Schools.* New York: Teachers College Press.

Olsen, L. (1997). *Made in America: Immigrant Students in Our Public Schools.* New York: The New Press.

Omi, M. and H. Winant. (1994). *Racial Formation in the United States: From the 1960s to the 1990s.* New York: Routledge.

Orellana, M.F. (2001). The work kids do: Mexican and Central American Children's Contributions to households and schools in California. *Harvard Educational Review, 71 (3),* 366-389.

Ovando, C. (2003). Bilingual education in the United States: Historical development and current issues. *Bilingual Research Journal, 27 (1),* 1-23.

Paredes, A. *Folklore and Culture on the Texas-Mexican Border.* Austin: Center for Mexican American Studies. 1993.

Painter, N.I. (2010). *The History of White People.* New York: Norton.

Parker, L., Deyhle, D., and Villenas, S., Eds. (1999). *Race Is, Race Ain't: Critical Race Theory and Qualitative Studies in Education.* Boulder, CO: Westview Press.

Perea, J.F. (2000). The Black/White Binary Paradigm of Race. In R. Delgado and J. Stefancic (Eds.) *Critical Race Theory : The Cutting Edge, 2nd Edition.* Philadelphia: Temple University Press.

Pérez, B. and M.E. Torres-Guzmán. *Learning in Two Worlds: An Integrated Spanish/English Biliteracy Approach.* New York: Longman, 1992.

Pérez-Torres, R. (1997). Nomads and Migrants: Negotiating a Multicultural Postmodernism. In Eds. Darder, Antonia, R. Torres and H. Gutiérrez. *Latinos and Education: A Critical Reader.* New York: Routledge.

Pérez, S. and Salazar, D. (1997). Economic, Labor Force, and Social Implications of Latino Educational and Population Trends. In

Eds., Darder, A., Torres, R. and Gutiérrez, H. *Latinos and Education: A Critical Reader*. New York: Routledge.

Po, R. (1998). The Racial Politics of Proposition 187. In Delgado, Richard and Jean Stefancic, eds. *The Latino/a Condition: A Critical Reader*. New York: New York University Press.

Portales, R. and M. (2005). *Quality Education for Latinos and Latinas: Print and Oral Skills for all Students, K-College.* Austin: University of Texas Press.

Portes, A. and R.C. Rumbaut. (2001). *Legacies: The Story of the Immigrant Second Generation*. Berkeley: University of California Press.

Ramirez, M.E. (2010) personal communication.

Reyes, M. and J.J. Halcón. (2001). *The Best for Our Children: Critical Perspectives on Literacy for Latino Students.* New York: Teachers College Press.

Salmons, J. and M. Wilkerson. (2008). "Good Old Immigrants of Yesteryear" Who Didn't Learn English: Germans in Wisconsin. *American Speech Vol. 83, No. 3*. San Miguel, G. (1987). *Let All of Them Take Heed: Mexican Americans and the Campaign for Educational Equality in Texas, 1910-1981*. Austin: University of Texas Press.

San Miguel, G., and Valencia, R.R. (1998). From the Treaty of Guadalupe Hidalgo to Hopwood: The educational plight and struggle of Mexican Americans in the southwest. *Harvard Educational Review 68*, 353-412.

Sánchez, G.J. (1993). *Becoming Mexican American: Ethnicity, Culture and Identity in Chicano* Los Angeles, 1900-1945. New York: Oxford University Press.

-(1997). History, Culture and Education. In A. Darder, R. Torres and H. Gutiérrez (Eds). *Latinos and Education: A Critical Reader*. New York: Routledge.

Schmidt, R., Sr. (2000). *Language Policy and Identity Politics in the United States*. Philadelphia: Temple University Press.

Skutnabb-Kangas, T. (1981). *Bilingualism or not? The education of minorities* (L. Malmberg and D. Crane, Trans.). Clevedon, UK: Multilingual Matters.

Sleeter, C. (2005). How White Teachers Construct Race. In C. McCarthy, W. Crichlow, G. Dimitriadis and N. Dolby (Eds.).

Race, Identity and Representation. 2nd Edition. New York: Taylor & Francis Group, LLC.

Solorzano, D. (1997). "Images and Words That Wound: Critical Race Theory, Racial Stereotyping, and Teacher Education." *Teacher Education Quarterly, 24,* 5-19.

Solorzano, D. Ceja, M. & Yosso, T.J. (2000). "Critical Race Theory, Racial Microaggressions and Campus Racial Climate: The Experiences of African American College Students." *Journal of Negro Education, 69,* 60-73.

-(2001). "Critical Race and LatCrit Theory and Method: Counterstorytelling Chicana and Chicano Graduate School Experiences." *International Journal of Qualitative Studies in Education, 14,* 471-495.

-(2009). Counter-Storytelling as an Analytical Framework for Educational Research. In Taylor, Edward, David Gillborn and Gloria Ladson-Billings, *Foundation of Critical Race Theory in Education.* New York: Routledge.

Solorzano, D. & Delgado Bernal, D. (2001). "Examining Transformational Resistance Through a Critical Race and LatCrit Theory Framework: Chicana and Chicano Students in an Urban Context." *Urban Education, 36,* 308-342.

Soto, L.D. (1997). *Language, culture and power: Bilingual families and the struggle for quality education.* Albany: State University of New York Press.

Stefancic, J. (1997). Latino and Latina Critical Theory: An Annotated Bibliography. *La Raza Law Journal 10*: 423-498.

Suárez-Orozco, C. and Suárez-Orozco, M. (2001). *Children of Immigration.* Cambridge, MA: The President and Fellows of Harvard College.

Suárez-Orozco, C., Suárez-Orozco, M. and Todorova, I. (2008) *Learning a New Land: Immigrant Students in American Society.* Cambridge, MA: The Belknap Press of the Harvard University Press.

Suárez-Orozco, M. (1989). *Central American Refugees and US High Schools: A Psychosocial Study of Motivation and Achievement.* Stanford, CA: Stanford University Press. - (1995). *Transformations: Immigration, Family Life and Achievement Motivation Among Latino Adolescents.* Stanford, CA: Stanford University Press.

- (1997). "Becoming Somebody": Central American Immigrants in US Inner-City Schools. In M. Seller and L. Weis, Eds. *Beyond Black and White: New Faces and Voices in US Schools.* Albany: State University of New York Press.

- (1998). Crossings; Mexican Immigration in Interdisciplinary Perspectives. In M. Suarez-Orozco, Ed *Crossings: Mexican Immigration in Interdisciplinary Perspectives.* Cambridge: The David Rockefeller Center Series on Latin American Studies.

Takaki, R. (1993). *A Different Mirror: A History of Multicultural America.* Boston: Little, Brown and Company.

Tate, W.F. (1995). Returning to the Root: A Culturally Relevant Approach to Mathematics Pedagogy. *Theory Into Practice*, Vol. 34, no. 3.

- (1997). Critical Race Theory and Education: History, Theory, and Implications. *Review of Research in Education, 22:* 195–247.

Tatum, B.D. (1997). *"Why Are All the Black Kids Sitting Together in the Cafeteria?"* New York: Basic Books.

Trucios-Haynes, E. Why "Race Matters": LatCrit Theory and Latino/a Racial Identity. *La Raza Law Journal, Vol 12:1.* 2001.

Trueba, E.T. (1998). "The Education of Mexican Immigrant Children" in M. Suárez-Orozco (Ed). *Crossings: Mexican Immigration in Interdisciplinary Perspectives.* Cambridge: The David Rockefeller Center Series on Latin American Studies.

Trujillo, A.L. (1998). *Chicano Empowerment and Bilingual Education: Movimiento Politics in Crystal City, Texas.* New York: Garland Publishing.

Ulluci, K. and D. Battey (2011). Exposing Color Blindness/Grounding Color Consciousness: Challenges for Teacher Education. *Urban Education, vol. 46, no. 6,* 1195-1225.

Valdés, F., McCristal Culp, J. and Harris, A.P. (2002). *Crossroads, Directions, and a New Critical Race Theory.* Philadelphia: Temple University Press.

Valdés, G. (1996). *Con Respeto, Bridging the Distance Between Culturally Diverse Families and Schools.* New York: Teachers College Press.

-(2001). *Learning and not learning English: Latino students in American schools.* New York: Teachers College Press.

Valencia, R.R. (2005). The Mexican American Struggle for Equal Educational Opportunity in Mendez v. Westminster: Helping to

Pave the Way for Brown v. Board of Education. *Teachers College Record 107: 3*, 389–423.

Valenzuela, A. (1999). *Subtractive Schooling: US-Mexican Youth and the Politics of Caring.* Albany: State University of New York Press.

Vargas, L. (2002). Latina/o-ization of the Midwest: Cambio de Colores (Change of Colors) as Agromaquilas Expand into the Heartland. *La Raza Legal Journal.*

Velez, V., Perez Huber, L., Benavides, C., de la Luz, A. & Solorzano, D. (2008). "Battling for Human rights and Social Justice: A Latina/o Critical Race Analysis of Latina/o Student Youth Activism in the Wake of 2006 Anti-Immigrant Sentiment." *Social Justice, 35*, 7-27.

Wallace, M. (1993). Multiculturalism and Oppositionality. In McCarthy, C.,W.Crichlow, Eds. *Race Identity and Representation in Education.* New York: Routledge.

Watkins, W.H., J.H. Lewis and V. Chou. (2001). *Race and Education: The Roles of History and Society in Educating African American Students.* Boston: Allyn and Bacon.

West, C. (1993). *Race Matters.* New York: Vintage.

Willis, P. (1977). *Learning to Labor: How Working Class Kids Get Working Class Jobs.* New York: Columbia University Press.

Winant, H. (1994). *Racial Conditions: Politics, Theory, Comparisons.* Minneapolis: University of Minnesota Press.

Wong Fillmore, L. (1991). When Learning a Second Language Means Losing the First. *Early Childhood Research Quarterly. Vol 6, Issue 3,* 323-346.

Woodson, C.G. (1933). *The Miseducation of the Negro.* Associated Publishers.

Yosso, T.J. (2006). *Critical Race Counterstories along the Chicana/Chicano Educational Pipeline.* New York: Routledge.

Yuval-Davis, N. (1997). *Gender and Nation.* London: Sage Publications.

Zinn, H. (2003). *A People's History of the United States: 1492-present.* 20th edition. NY: HarperCollins.

Index

CPSIA information can be obtained at www.ICGtesting.com
Printed in the USA
BVOW03*2156260314

348816BV00004B/150/P